The Scholarship Docto

5 Easy Steps To A **FREE** Degree

By: Rhea M. Watson,
The Scholarship Doctor

The Traveling Toddler Publishing Company

ISBN-13: 978-1-7356243-2-7

"The world is waiting for you. You got this!"

-Scholarship Doctor

DEDICATION

This book is dedicated to Mr. Edward Lewis Watson, my father, and Mrs. Cynthia Watson, my beautiful mother. Yearly, for about five years, Daddy asked, “Rhee, when are you going to write that book?” I can boldly say, “Daddy, it’s done.” A heavenly thanks for the confidence, Daddy. Mama, thanks for being the most amazing prayer warrior, biggest cheerleader, and most precious confidant. I love you both.

My parents taught me hard work and true work ethic. I was and am a true Daddy’s Girl. Everything my Daddy taught me will live to guide and direct as his words, lessons, and encouragement continue to inspire my passion and what I am purposed to do.

I would be remiss not to express my love and gratitude for my beautiful sister, Racquel Watson Boumah. My superbly supportive Brother-in-Love, Joseph Boumah, and my handsome, amazing and intelligent nephew, Justyn Boumah. All of you -- Dad, Mom, Sister, Brother, and Nephew, have told me there is a way and that you will help me find it.

Lastly, I want to dedicate this book to every scholar whose life I have had the opportunity to impact through Scholarship Solutions. May you continue to grow and excel, not only academically, but in every aspect of your life.

Thank you - Everyone - Really.

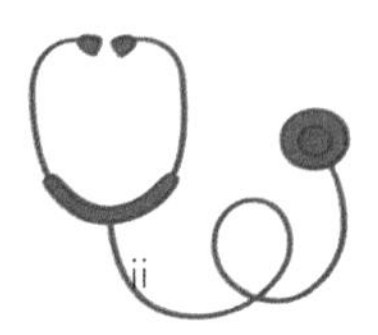

"My child goes to college for **FREE**!"

-Grateful Parent

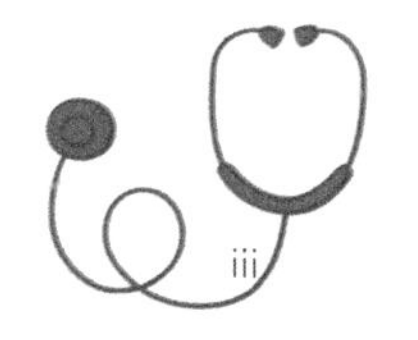

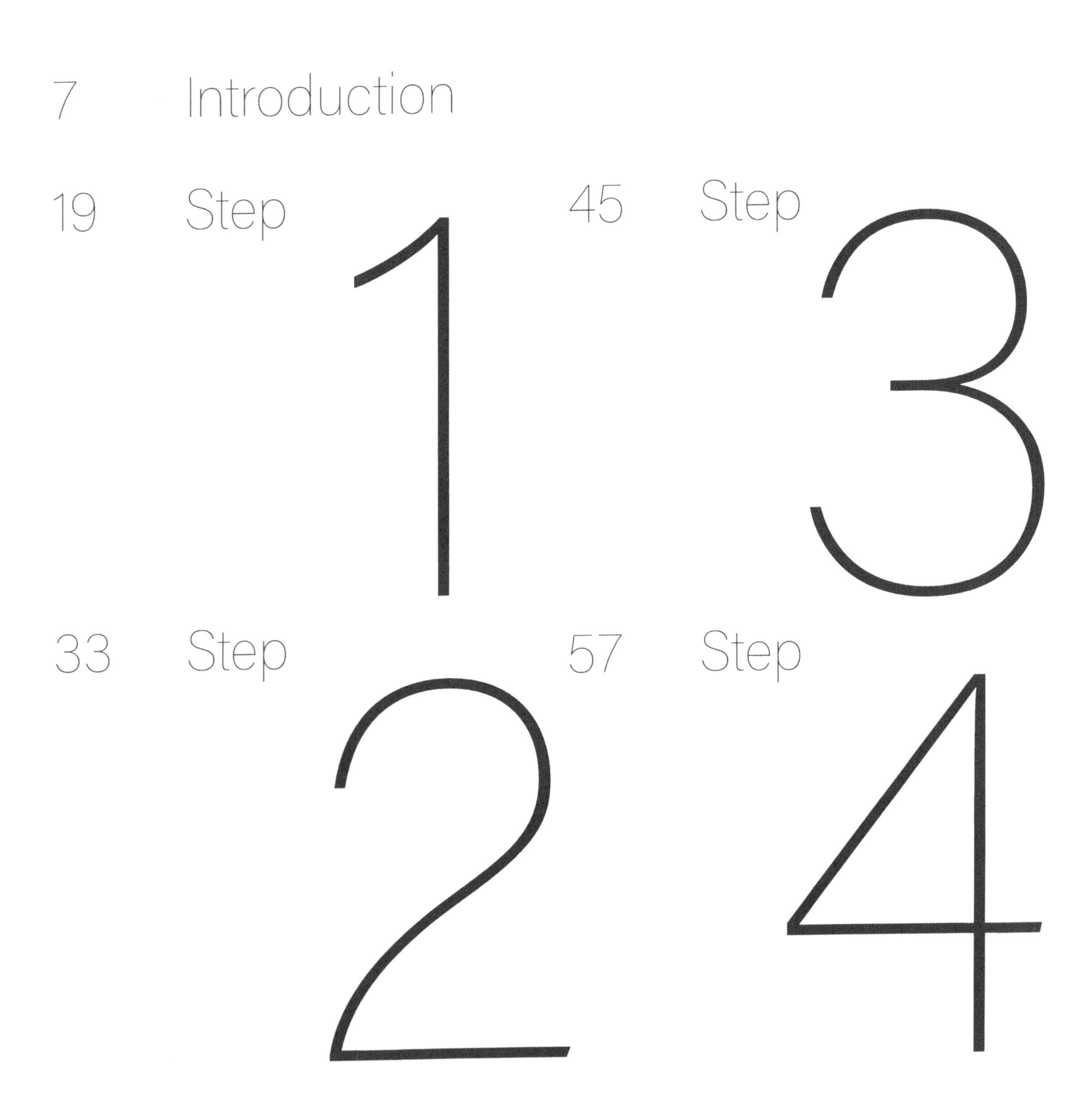

"Start earning scholarships at birth."

- Scholarship Doctor

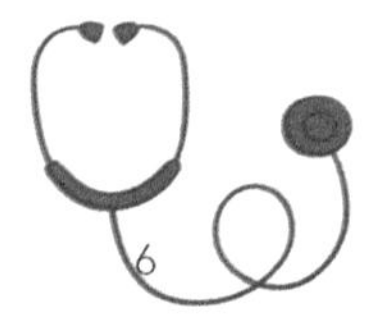

INTRODUCTION

My dad always told me, "Do what you don't want to do now, so you can do what you want to do later." This is an important consideration when jumping into the scholarship game. As your Scholarship Doctor, I am keenly aware it is not always easy to apply, apply, apply for scholarships. However, it is simple and doing so can and will bring huge rewards.

Additionally, more often than not, people are misinformed about the process of applying for scholarships. Often, students stand a better chance than they realize and therefore are incredibly qualified for many of the scholarships offered. It is my intent to encourage and inspire you to go on a quest in obtaining a debt-free degree with me, Rhee, the Scholarship Doctor and the help of Scholarship Solutions.

So, let's talk about the myths and misconceptions that may stop you from applying for scholarships.

Scholarship Myths

Students do not always follow through with the process of applying for scholarships because of some of the myths that exist. The following are a few of the popular misconceptions regarding the scholarship process:

- **You should begin researching and applying for scholarships during senior year:** The scholarship search and application processes should begin today. There are a myriad of scholarships for students of various ages, educational, and learning levels. Specifically, the scholarship processes can begin as early as birth. There is surely a prescription to successfully obtaining scholarships; that is

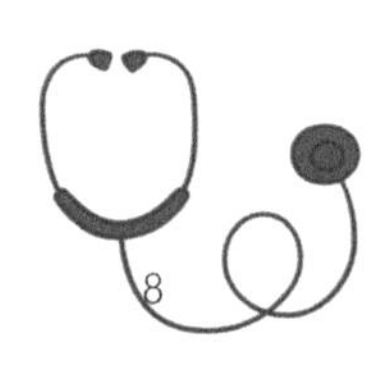

why you are reading this book, right? However, the mantra to live by in the scholarship space is early and often, early and often, early and often. You will see this saying throughout the book. Consequently, the earlier you start your scholarship research and application processes, the better your chances of earning scholarships and avoiding student loan debt. Please, do not only focus on senior year to start searching for, applying to, or earning college scholarships -- start today. No matter your age, educational level, nationality, or the like. Your time for scholarships is NOW.

- **Scholarships are only obtained by top scholars and students who are athletes:** This is a myth for sure. There are just as many scholarships for academics as there are for athletics, if not more. Additionally, there are scholarships based on the Three M's: Merit, Music, and Miscellaneous Components. Merit scholarships are based on your volunteer efforts and what you have done outside of the classroom, such as being involved with clubs and community-based organizations. Music-based scholarships can come from a college or university, as well as a scholarship organization like the Jack Kent Cooke Young Artist Award (See **Chapter 8** for scholarship details) which focuses on scholars ages 8 to 18 who are composers, musicians, and vocalists. Miscellaneous Components include attributes and character traits such as: Ethnicity, Religion, Location, Language, Grade Level or College Classification, College Major, Ability, and so many other areas. Therefore, there are all types of scholarships that do not consider grade point average or athletic ability as a foundation or consideration when applying for or receiving free college funding.

- **You have to be an extraordinary essay writer:** This is not true. Often, it is more about what you write rather than how well it is written. Using creativity, sharing a unique quote, and having the discipline to follow the guidelines and the ability to address the essay questions appropriately, will often yield more success than an eloquent piece of writing.
- **You must be a high school student to obtain a scholarship:** This is another falsehood. There are scholarships available for all ages, students, non-students, ethnic groups, and the like. You do not have to be a high school student to qualify. In fact, scholarship committees love to see diversity. So, an application from a senior citizen or nontraditional student will surely stand out, perhaps helping to increase your scholarship chances. Additionally, there are scholarships for students ages 0 to 99 so you are never too young or young at heart to win at the scholarship game. Moreover, although there are plenty of scholarships for students, you truly do not have to be one to earn scholarships. So, are you looking to increase revenue in your business? Do you have a goal to start a non-profit organization or do you want to begin a new degree? If so, look for scholarships and other funding options like pitch competitions or pageants that can and will pay you handsomely, and

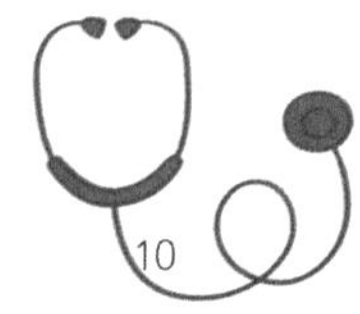

you do not, I repeat, you do not, have to be a student.

- **Most of the scholarships are not worth applying for because the award amounts are small:** Every dollar counts! Multiple awards of $500 or $1000 can quickly add up to one $10,000 scholarship and make a huge difference in your opportunity to attend the school of your choice and to do so debt free. Do not in any way look down on the smaller amounts. One of my favorite scholarships is for those who are juniors in high school through graduate/professional students. It is called the Courage to Grow Scholarship (See **Chapter 8** for scholarship details). This scholarship awards students $500 and they do so on a monthly basis. Although the scholarship is not a huge award, winning this scholarship does so many things. For example, A) It adds to your scholarship winnings, meaning there is one less dollar out of your pocket, savings, or household budget. B) It is an award you can use to win other scholarships. C) It gives you the opportunity to use an award-winning essay for other scholarship competitions both large and small. So apply for everything and watch those smaller dollar amounts add up to a debt-free degree.
- **Finding scholarships is very time consuming and most times you don't qualify for what you find:** It does take time and tenacity to search for scholarships. If research is not your strong suit, this is surely where a scholarship specialist can assist in finding scholarships that fit your academic, social, ethnic, religious, and

other profiles. Therefore, once the research has been completed and you have scholarships that are specifically catered to your needs, you can simply follow the application instructions, pay close attention to the required information and due date, apply, and win scholarships. The time that you spend applying and the dollars that you are awarded matters and makes a difference. Remember, this is free money which you do not have to pay back. So research the funding or invest in a professional service that can provide you with the desired information. Either option, searching on your own or working with a professional, will be worth the investment of time and/or money.

- **The scholarship application is a one-time thing:** Not true. There are scholarship dollars available daily, weekly, monthly, and yearly. Sometimes awards are one time. However, there are awards you can apply for each year or some which are automatically renewed. It is important to understand how a particular scholarship works. A scholarship specialist can help you wade through these processes.
- **Volunteering does not help you to obtain scholarships:** Not true. Your involvement in the community and working with organizations that give back to the community is one of the best methods to help catapult your success story when applying for scholarships. The volunteer activities you participate in are not important. Honestly, you can and should give back in a myriad of unique and helpful ways. However, your involvement should be, whenever possible: **creative, consistent,**

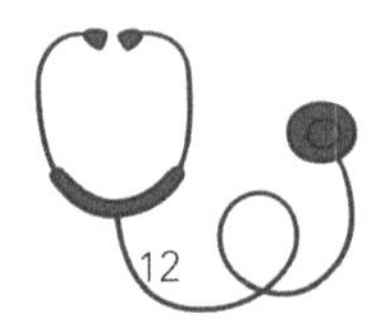

community-minded. Plain and simple, Volunteerism = Scholarships.

- **Testing is not important when applying for scholarships:** Strong test scores in regard to applying for scholarships are not only important but necessary. Do not believe the myth that you are limited to how many times you can take the exam or concerned it looks "bad" to scholarship or college admissions committees if you have multiple scores. The truth is one should test as early and often as possible to perfect the skill of testing and to increase your opportunity to be awarded funds at the highest levels. Additionally, taking a test prep course to help increase test-taking strategies and skills will only help to bring in big scholarship dollars. At Scholarship Solutions, we have always worked to have quality test prep courses. Furthermore, we believe test prep and taking the PSAT/ACT/SAT exams should begin as early as age 10. Consequently, starting at this age, scholars will surely secure the scores they need by summer of junior year.
- **I can do this by myself:** Of course people win scholarships without the help of a professional. However, having a scholarship specialist to help you navigate through the scholarship process, the instructions of applications, the brainstorming and editing of essays, and much more, is the next best thing to having the money in hand. Be open for help and I, as the Scholarship Doctor, and my team at Scholarship Solutions, have created so many options to help you win big at the scholarship game! So we, through this book, our Scholarship

Solutions Membership, VIP services, social media pages, and speaking engagements, are here to help you earn a free degree.

The above are just a few examples of myths regarding scholarships. Scholarship Solutions was created on the foundation of seeing every deserving and aspiring student who desires to attend college has the opportunity to go for FREE!! It is a proven fact, with effort and consistency, the goal of earning a debt-free degree is possible. Consequently, Scholarship Solutions is committed to assisting you in defusing any scholarship myths. Our goal is to help provide a prescription for overcoming the myths and to show you the steps to successfully applying for and winning scholarships so you can have a degree debt-free!

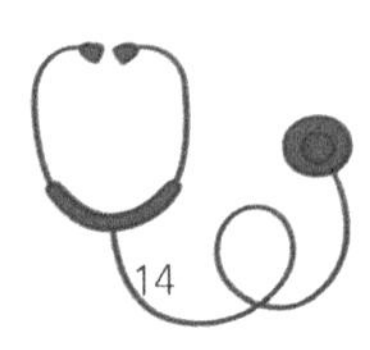

"I won 1 million dollars in schol-arships even in a **gap** year!"

- Gap Year Student

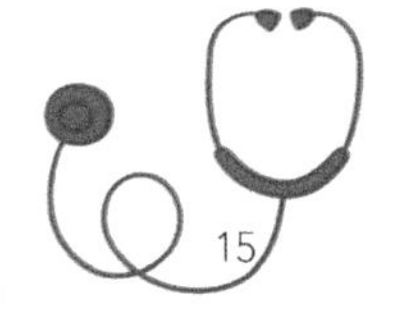

NOW LET'S FILL THE PRESCRIPTION

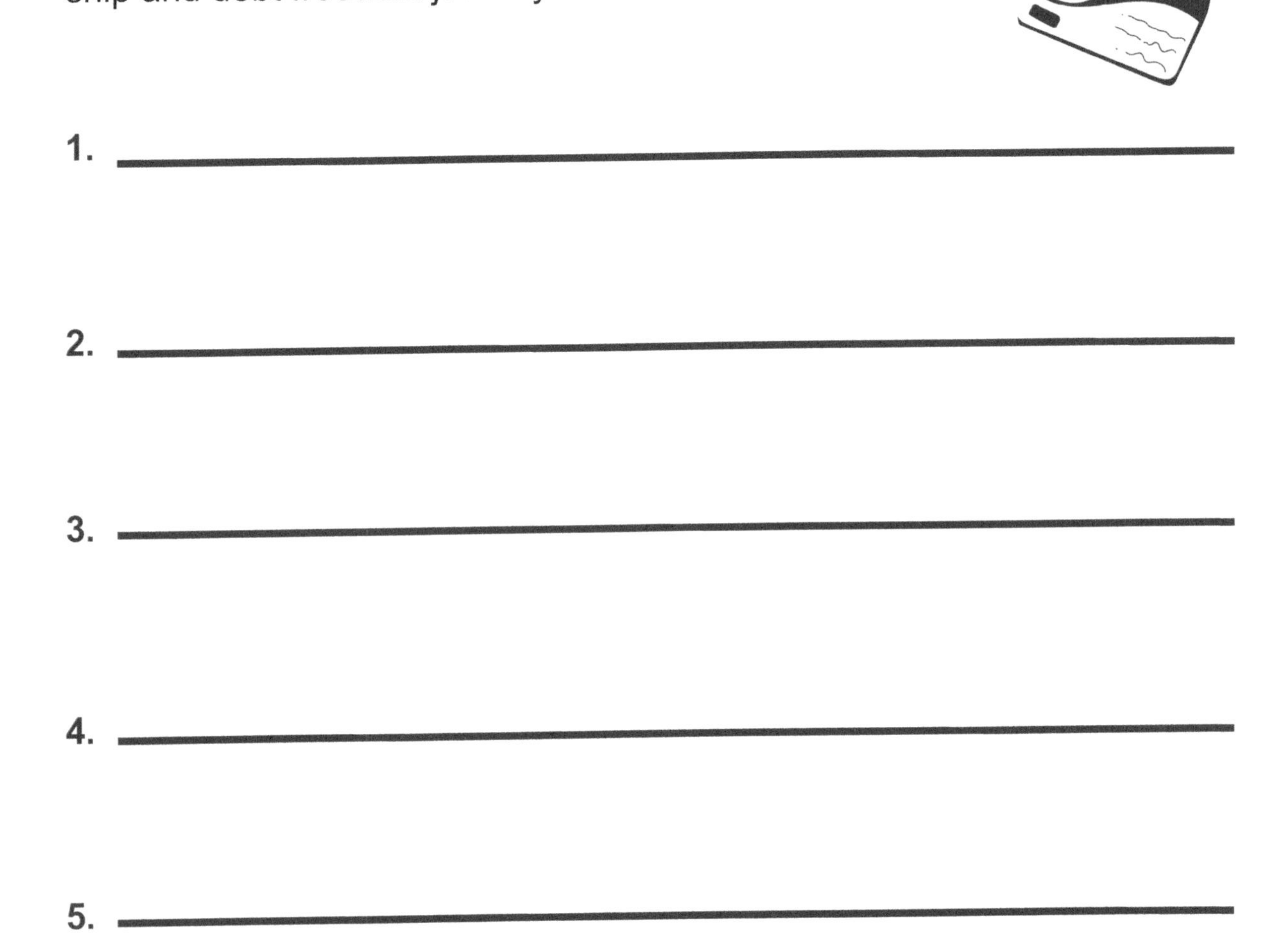

What personal myths do you have to overcome before starting your scholarship and debt freedom journey?

1. ______________________________

2. ______________________________

3. ______________________________

4. ______________________________

5. ______________________________

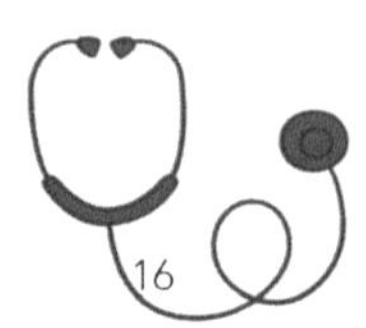

NOW LET'S FILL THE PRESCRIPTION

Name 5 things you plan on doing to dispel the myths in your life.

1. ______________________________

2. ______________________________

3. ______________________________

4. ______________________________

5. ______________________________

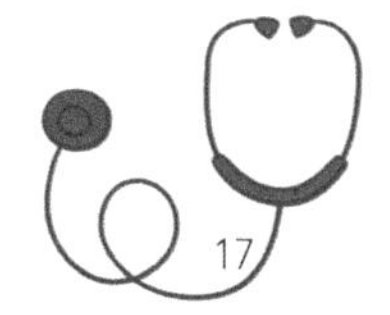

"Take a deep breath."

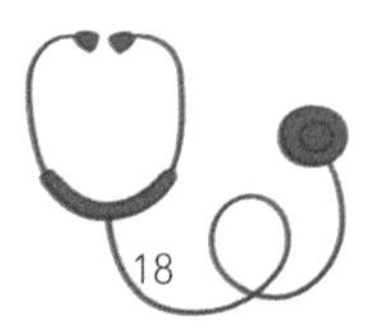

- Scholarship Doctor

1

Step One: Great **GPA**

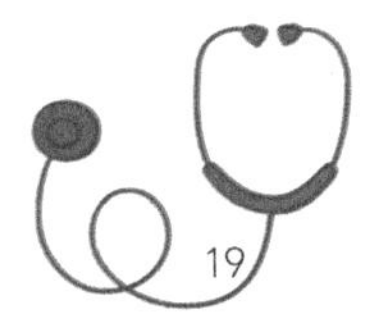

Let's Talk GPA

Although the "A" student is not the only ideal candidate for scholarships, a great grade point average (GPA) should never be ignored. To be more specific, if you have a 4.0 GPA, that is great! We love it! However, if you only have good grades and nothing else on your resume, it is not the required balance scholarship funders are seeking. Yet again, grades and GPA should be stellar, just make sure they are not the only areas in which you excel.

So you may be wondering, what is a great GPA? You should minimally have a cumulative GPA of 3.8. That is all As and one B. This is overall, not just for one or two semesters. Additionally, the cumulative GPA is particularly relative to high school students. More specifically, this is the GPA without any additional weight. Traditionally, Honor, Advanced Placement (AP), International Baccalaureate (IB), and sometimes Dual Credit (where you are enrolled in college classes and receive credit at both the high school and college levels), classes provide additional points or weight to the GPA. Therefore, for example, someone who has a cumulative GPA/unweighted GPA of 4.0 could possibly have a weighted GPA of 4.8 or higher. Although we love the weighted GPA, it is important that your cumulative/unweighted GPA is 3.8. Normally, this means a student's weighted GPA is a bit higher at 4.2. Recently, I had a discussion with an Assistant Director of Admissions at a major state university. I explained my client was interested in transferring to their school and wanted information about their scholarship opportunities. The director informed me that a 3.7 GPA was borderline for scholarships and they could not guarantee receipt of money with that GPA. Our discussion brought me full circle that everyone, regardless of educational level - elementary, middle school, high school, or college - should have a minimum GPA of 3.8. In fact, there is a scholarship organization that supports students in grades 4 through 11. They celebrate scholars with high grades and community involvement (See **Step Four: Excellent Volunteer History** for more details regarding the importance of giving back to your community). The scholarship is sponsored by Former United States Secretary of Housing and Urban Development and Retired Neurosurgeon, Dr. Ben Carson. This outstanding scholarship honors students with a 3.75 GPA or greater with a $1,000 scholarship, a medallion, and a trophy. Check out this unique scholarship opportunity in **Chapter 8**.

Now, I do not want you to close the book and walk away because you may not have a 3.8 GPA. Please know there are many scholarships that do not require a GPA, or the points required may be lower than my recommendation. However, to be the most competitive, especially for scholarships in the 10s and 100s of thousands of dollars range, the key is to have a great cumulative GPA of 3.8 or higher. If this is not your current narrative, change it. I have helped hundreds of scholars to become "A" and "A" students. In fact, it is my superpower - helping students to change "Fs" to "As". So, do not be dismayed, start working on "A" grades and a great GPA today and always.

Tutoring is for Everyone

We have already discussed the importance of earning good grades and maybe you are trying to figure out how to turn your current GPA into something higher, therefore increasing your scholarship chances. Well, at Scholarship Solutions we believe in order to help achieve A grades, one should take full advantage of tutoring services available at your school, college, public library, community organization, or a private company like mine.

Using the services and experiences of a tutor will help raise and maintain grades. Tutors really should be a part of what I like to call the "Scholarship Dream Team." Every scholar starting as early as Pre-K should have a team with these members: an Athletic Coach, an Artistic Teacher, a Tutor, a Test Prep Instructor, and a Scholarship Specialist. This dream team will provide students with the opportunity to be challenged to do above average and to excel in every area of life. This is important because it can help to provide 10s to 100s of thousands of dollars in scholarship offers. Also, we sometimes have the idea tutors should be used when we are struggling with a subject. However, this is not the correct frame of thought. For example, one of my clients had been receiving regular tutoring since 3rd grade. Because tutoring was such a natural part of their lives, when the scholar was in high school and college they continued with this incredible habit and excelled over and over again. Moreover, this scholar became a semi-finalist with the coveted National Merit Scholarship Corporation (See **Chapter 8** for scholarship details). This status provided the scholar with multiple full ride scholarship offers to elite colleges and universities. They were also placed in a special pool of scholarship applicants because of their status as a semi-finalist with National Merit. This students commitment to tutoring to help maintain "A" grades, stay ahead in classes, and prepare for standardized tests like the PSAT/ACT/SAT (we will learn more about National Merit Scholarships and PSAT/ACT/SAT in **Step 3: Great PSAT/ACT/SAT Scores)**, helped them to earn a degree in record time and earn scholarships to do so. Therefore, tutors should be involved with the learning process from the beginning to help avoid struggles in particular subjects. Tutors help to build confidence and assure that homework assignments are completed correctly the first time. See, we all start with a 100%, A grades, and perfect scores. When working with a tutor, regularly, we are able to maintain "A" status. So please know and live by this principle, "tutoring is for smart people". Anyone who wants to be successful in their scholarship quest should add tutoring as a part of their college and scholarship plans.

"...she has helped us to **focus** and has given us clarity"

-Focused & Funded

"Our baby was **only** 4-months old when she said apply. So we did!"

-Parents of a Baby Scholar

NOW LET'S FILL THE PRESCRIPTION

☐ I have selected a tutor.

Tutor Name & Subject

Tutor Name & Subject

Tutor Name & Subject

Tutor Name & Subject

Tutor Name & Subject

Tutor Name & Subject

Tutor Name & Subject

Tutor Name & Subject

Tutor Name & Subject

Tutor Name & Subject

Tutor Name & Subject

Tutor Name & Subject

Tutor Name & Subject

Tutor Name & Subject

Tutor Name & Subject

Tutoring Schedule:

Challenging Subjects:

Current 1st Semester Grades:

Current 2nd Semester Grades:

☐ I know my cumulative (unweighted) GPA.

Previous Cumulative GPA/Date: ____________________

Current Cumulative GPA/Date: ____________________

Previous Cumulative GPA/Date: ____________________

Current Cumulative GPA/Date: ____________________

Previous Cumulative GPA/Date: ____________________

Current Cumulative GPA/Date: ____________________

☐ I know my weighted GPA.

Previous Weighted GPA/Date: ____________________

Current Weighted GPA/Date: ____________________

Previous Weighted GPA/Date: ____________________

Current Weighted GPA/Date: ____________________

Previous Weighted GPA/Date: ____________________

Current Weighted GPA/Date: ____________________

NOW LET'S APPLY WHAT WE LEARNED

I will make the following changes:

1. ______________________________

____

____

2. ______________________________

____

____

3. ______________________________

____

____

THE PROGRESS SO FAR

The changes I made gave me these results:

1. ______________________________

____

____

2. ______________________________

____

____

3. ______________________________

____

____

"Trust the process. Don't give up and don't give in."

- Scholarship Doctor

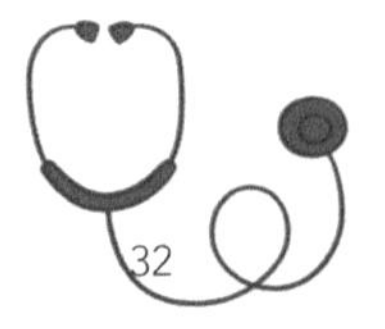

Step Two: Great **Class Rank**

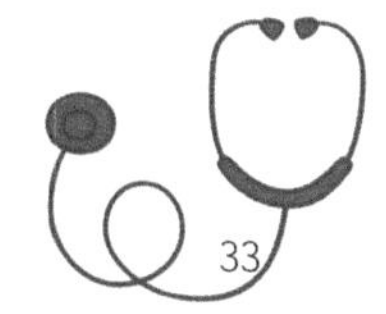

Rank Up

Class rank is important. Your class rank is how you are placed academically versus everyone else in your graduating class. The closer you are to the number one spot in your class, the greater the opportunity to earn huge scholarships. Amazingly, there are scholarships available for those who are ranked in the top 5% and 10% of their graduating classes. There are also scholarships for persons who graduate as valedictorian (Number 1) or salutatorian (Number 2). To take advantage of scholarships in correlation with your class rank, contact your state colleges and universities. State schools love to "grow their own" so they will reward you handsomely, scholarship-wise, if you finish top of your class. However, there are college and scholarship programs that do not require state residency. Check out some of these programs for scholars who finish number one, two, or are ranked at the top of their graduating classes. I think it is so exciting to know your hard work and great grades can pay off, incredibly, with you winning scholarships for no other reason than going to school and doing well in your classes.

1. **Abilene Christian University Valedictorian/Salutatorian**
2. **Aquinas College Valedictorian**
3. **Clemson Scholars Award**
4. **Grace College Valedictorian/Salutatorian Scholarship**
5. **Great Bay Community College New Hampshire Valedictorian Scholarship**

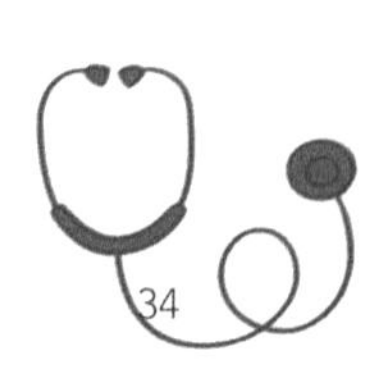

So, the moral of this scholarship story is you want to finish at the top of your class, no matter the educational level from Kindergarten to graduate school. Ranking in the highest percentiles will transform into hundreds of thousands of dollars in scholarship offers from colleges and universities as well as independent scholarship organizations.

Choose the Correct Classes

Having a great GPA and high class rank are the first steps to winning at the scholarship game. In addition to these important steps are choosing classes that will show you are college bound. More specifically, the types of classes you take can be a direct reflection on your class ranking. Therefore, high school students should take the most difficult classes you are able to handle and attend school for the full day, especially as a graduating high school senior. So many times, I see high school seniors who have decided to **"take senior year off."** Senior year is not the year to take a break. It should be the very opposite. Senior year is the time to show a college/university/scholarship you are the hardest working and most dedicated student on the planet. Now, if you are reading this book and you have taken the lowest math class offered or you are taking multiple unnecessary electives, have your schedule changed to reflect your academic abilities, demonstrating to any college or scholarship that you are ready to take on the challenge of college life. College is about hard work, discipline, and time management. Developing these habits while in middle school and high school are important elements to becoming and transitioning into being a college student and highly rewarded scholarship recipient.

Counselors Care

Middle School, High School, Undergraduate, and Graduate students should meet with their counselors regularly. Middle school students, you can learn about cool classes to take, unique opportunities at school, scholarships and more. High school students, you can find about colleges, scholarships, classes, and clubs. Undergraduate and Graduate students, your academic and or financial aid counselors may have information about internships, graduation plans, scholarships, fellowships, etc. Therefore, meeting with your counselor whether they are your high school or college counselor, career coach, track coordinator, academic advisor, or scholarship coach, will help you graduate at the top of your class while avoiding the detriment of debt. Conversations with Counselors = Debt Free Degrees.

Ten Transcripts

The best way to stay on track with your class rank and grades is by your transcript. Your transcript lists your grades, class rank, classes, graduation information, and more. Talk to your counselor or registrar's office about obtaining two unofficial and ten official copies of your transcript. Having multiple copies of your official transcript will help assure you are prepared to apply for internships, get accepted to colleges, and earn scholarships.

"At one point, I was applying for **twenty** scholarships per week."

-College Paid in Full

NOW LET'S FILL THE PRESCRIPTION

☐ I have met with my counselor.

My counselor(s) is: ______________________________

Initial Meeting Date/Notes: ______________________________

____

____

______________________ ______________________

Next Meeting Date Next Meeting Date

☐ I know my class rank.

Previous Class Rank: ______________________

Current Class Rank: ______________________

Previous Class Rank: ______________________

Current Class Rank: ______________________

☐ I have 2 unofficial transcripts.

______________________	______________________
End of 1st Semester Date Received	End of 2nd Semester Date Received
______________________	______________________
End of 1st Semester Date Received	End of 2nd Semester Date Received

☐ I have 10 official transcripts.

______________________	______________________
End of 1st Semester Date Received	End of 2nd Semester Date Received
______________________	______________________
End of 1st Semester Date Received	End of 2nd Semester Date Received

☐ I have selected my classes for this semester.

Class/Tutor Needed Y or N	Class/Tutor Needed Y or N
Class/Tutor Needed Y or N	Class/Tutor Needed Y or N
Class/Tutor Needed Y or N	Class/Tutor Needed Y or N
Class/Tutor Needed Y or N	Class/Tutor Needed Y or N
Class/Tutor Needed Y or N	Class/Tutor Needed Y or N
Class/Tutor Needed Y or N	Class/Tutor Needed Y or N
Class/Tutor Needed Y or N	Class/Tutor Needed Y or N
Class/Tutor Needed Y or N	Class/Tutor Needed Y or N

Future Classes:

Future Challenging Classes:

NOW LET'S APPLY WHAT WE LEARNED

I will make the following changes:

1. ____________________

____

____

2. ____________________

____

____

3. ____________________

____

____

THE PROGRESS SO FAR

The changes I made gave me these results:

1. ______________________________

____

____

2. ______________________________

____

____

3. ______________________________

____

____

"Test Prep is necessary!"

- Scholarship Doctor

Step Three: Great **PSAT/ACT/ SAT Scores**

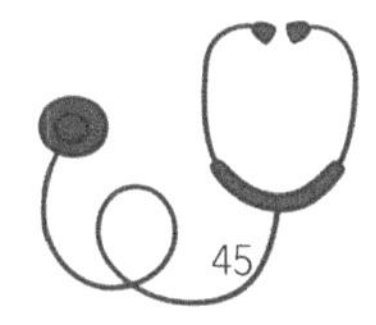

Take Tests

The ACT and SAT exams are critical for entering college and for securing scholarships. As you may have heard, some colleges are exploring the "Test Optional" world. However, you must realize it is an option. So, just like you can opt out, you can also opt in. Also, although there may be some flexibility of not having or needing test scores for admissions, this is rarely the case for scholarships. Therefore, in order to be the most competitive for scholarships from your top choice institutions as well as large and small scholarships, optimal test scores are an absolute necessity.

Currently, the ACT and SAT exams are being offered practically every month. So, there is no excuse for not taking the test early and often. Specifically, prepare thoroughly for the ACT and SAT exams in order to help increase your scholarship earnings. Statistics show, for every point you increase on the ACT exam, which is equivalent to about 40 points on the SAT, your scholarship options also increase by $25,000 on average. I have seen one point on the ACT test make the difference between a full and partial academic scholarship. Consequently, you should invest time and energy in obtaining the best score(s) possible on these tests. It is highly encouraged that you take a test prep class, study through programs provided by your school, borrow study materials from the library, take an online or in person test prep course from my company, Scholarship Solutions, or one of my colleagues in the field. Truly, test preparation, practice, planning, and praying can pay off greatly in regard to college acceptances and scholarship offerings.

Three Times and That's All Folks

I have heard a myriad of untruths in regard to the ACT and SAT exams. Incorrect notions like, "You can only take ACT/SAT three times," "You can only take the test once, "If you take the test more than three times - Harvard won't accept you," "You know taking the test more than three times makes you look 'dumb', so don't do that," "Wait until the summer of your junior year in high school to take ACT/SAT exams." Unfortunately, these falsehoods have students trapped into believing "perfect scores" must be solidified in a one and done manner. Actually, this belief could not be further from the truth. Additionally, students create the belief they have to be super test-takers and do everything on their own, having the fogged perception that taking a test prep course or using study materials to prepare equates to them not being "smart or versed enough" in the materials being covered on the exam. These methodologies will create a world of debt for scholars. Please do not believe the hype that you must be a martyr in the ACT/SAT test-taking processes. Instead, you should take this approach when planning to take either the ACT or the SAT exam:

1. **Take ACT and SAT Exams Early and Often.** As discussed, some of the most important pieces to your college and scholarship application puzzles are strong standardized test scores. You want to earn a score as close to perfect as possible on these tests. To achieve optimal scores you want to start at least in 9th grade, and take them multiple times in a year. Optimal scores of 1400 on the SAT

and 30 on the ACT are what scholarship funders are seeking in order to award maximum scholarship dollars.

2. Take a test prep course. After students have taken a quality test prep course, on average, their scores increase by 4 points on the ACT and 160 points on the SAT. Please remember, for every one point you increase on the ACT and every 40 points on the SAT, you have the potential to increase your scholarship winnings by $25,000. Scholarship Solutions has provided quality online ACT/SAT test prep courses for years. We would be happy to have you as a part of our courses, the scholarship benefits are worth the investment!

3. Study, Study, Study. Make test preparation a regular part of your study schedule. Read, study vocabulary, go over math facts, and really prepare for the exam. When it comes to music, athletics, or dance, no one who wants to be successful goes in to a game or recital unprepared. Multiple practices, poignant training, and lots of time are put into helping secure success in these areas. Take the same approach when it comes to the ACT/SAT. Give it your all both inside and outside of class time. When you put in the diligent and quality study time, you will help increase scores and increase your scholarship chances

PSAT

PSAT, also known as the Pre-SAT and/or Practice SAT, is a scholarship exam. More specifically, on the second Wednesday in October, this exam is offered in correlation with the National Merit Scholarship Program. The scholarship competition occurs during students' junior year and is awarded in senior year. However, although junior year is the year that it "counts" for scholarships, it is surely not the only time one should take the test.

Applying the same philosophy as discussed for ACT/SAT, one should take the exam early and often. In my professional opinion, students should begin the test-taking process in 6th Grade. Why? Because, by the time it truly matters, in 11th Grade, students will be thoroughly prepared and therefore will help secure the scores needed to successfully compete for the National Merit Scholarship.

Why am I so passionate about students taking the PSAT? Well, there are a few reasons. First, when middle school students have strong scores on the PSAT exam, they have access to incredible academic programs like:

1. **Duke TIP**
2. **Cornell CAU Youth Program**
3. **Vanderbilt Program for Talented Youth**

Second, there are tons of scholarship opportunities. Specifically, the National Merit Scholarship Program supports $2,500 scholarships. Also, they have a multitude of corporate sponsors who award scholarships. However, most amazingly, some of the largest scholarships are funded by colleges and universities who offer National Merit semifinalists and finalists partially and fully funded scholarships. Some examples of colleges where you can receive amazing scholarship offers in correlation with being a National Merit finalist are:

1. **University of Alabama: Full Ride + $6K Stipend**
2. **Oakwood University: Full Ride**
3. **Arizona State University: Full Tuition**
4. **Florida State University: Full Ride + Books**
5. **University of Texas at Dallas: Full Tuition + 11K Stipend**

As you can see, the PSAT is game changer in regard to the availability of scholarships. Therefore, please take the exam early and often, study, prepare, and practice so that you can be among the top 1% of test-takers. In doing so, you can write your ticket to debt freedom and not only attend college for free, but get PAID to attend school. It is 100% possible and students all over the world secure this incredible accomplishment every year.

Although this chapter has widely focused on students who are in middle and high school, if you are a college student seeking a graduate degree, you need strong test scores, too. Thoroughly prepare for your graduate entrance exams and start your study plan no later than your junior year in college. Your course of action should also include test prep courses, a dedicated study plan, and a commitment to taking your required tests multiple times in order to reach your needed scores.

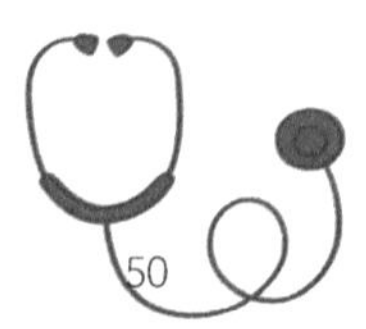

"Rhea has been a **HUGE** help to my family!"

- Happy Family

NOW LET'S FILL THE PRESCRIPTION

☐ I have registered for the PSAT at my local High School.

PSAT Score & Date:

6th- ____________________ 9th- ____________________

7th- ____________________ 10th- ____________________

8th- ____________________ 11th- ____________________

☐ I have registered for the ACT at www.act.org.

ACT Score & Date:

6th- ____________________ 9th- ____________________

7th- ____________________ 10th- ____________________

8th- ____________________ 11th- ____________________

☐ I have registered for the SAT at www.collegeboard.org.

SAT Score & Date:

6th- ____________________ 9th- ____________________

7th- ____________________ 10th- ____________________

8th- ____________________ 11th- ____________________

☐ I have registered for Graduate School Entance Exams.

Test Score & Date:

1st- ____________________ 2nd- ____________________

My top three colleges & scholarship requirements.

1. ____

2. ____

3. ____

NOW LET'S APPLY WHAT WE LEARNED

I will make the following changes:

1. ______________________________

____

____

2. ______________________________

____

____

3. ______________________________

____

____

THE PROGRESS SO FAR

The changes I made gave me these results:

1. ______________________________

____

____

2. ______________________________

____

____

3. ______________________________

____

____

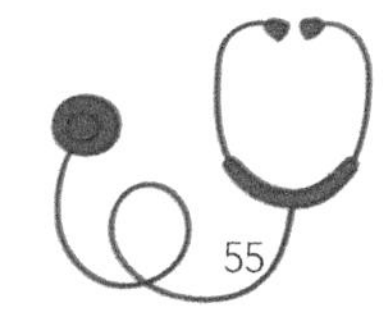

"A surefire way NOT to win a scholarship: Don't apply!"

- Scholarship Doctor

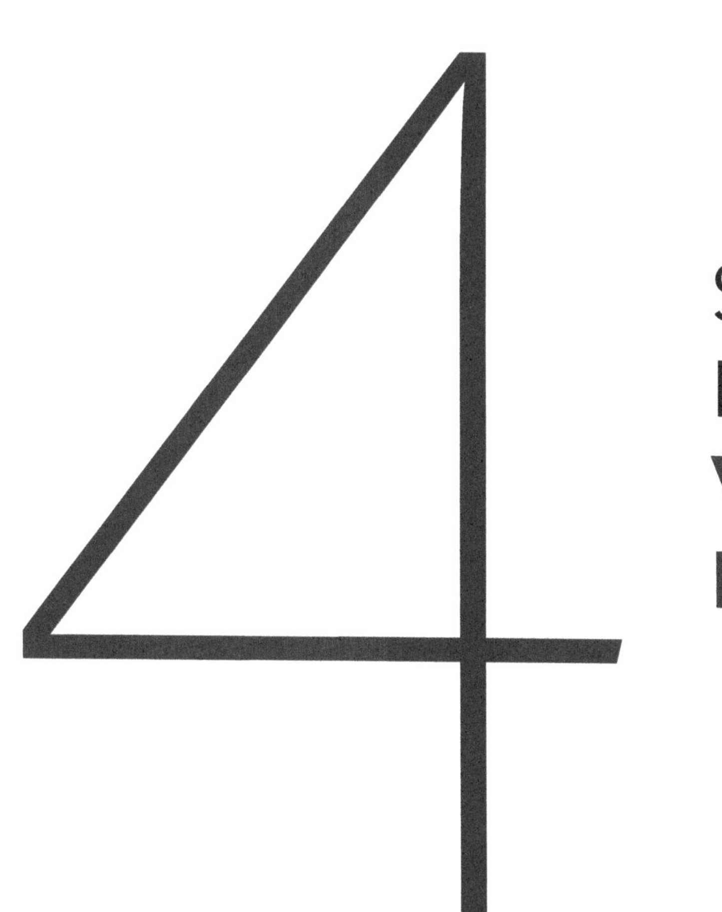

Step Four: EXCELLENT **VOLUNTEER HISTORY**

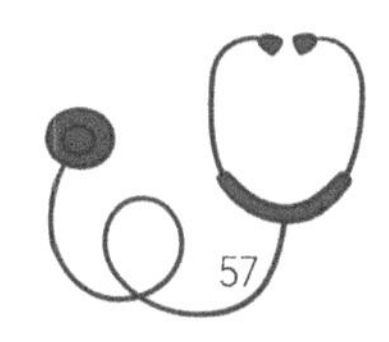

My Daddy was a huge community servant. As a result, his compassion and passion for volunteerism surely flowed to my sister and me. In fact, he said, "I work. You volunteer." Because of my wonderful Dad and Mom, we were committed to volunteering throughout our beautiful Las Vegas community. In return, we earned 1000s of dollars in scholarships. Therefore, volunteerism is vital to earning scholarship dollars. When volunteering, it should be fun! Do something you enjoy. As a volunteer,you can work with animals, veterans, at your place of worship, the library, or in a community garden. The opportunities are endless. When you volunteer, you feel great and scholarship organizations recognize your service in a big way!

Everyone Needs a Little R and R

So far, we have discussed the academic portions of earning scholarship dollars. However, that is not the whole picture when it comes to winning big at the scholarship game. In fact, although A and A grades and strong test scores are very important, grades and scores should not be the only contributors to your scholarship applications. Specifically, every student needs R and R! What is R and R? It is a Robust Resume. A Robust Resume is especially important for what is known as the merit-based scholarship. Merit scholarships consider the actions and activities of students in addition to grades and scores. Moreover, there are millions of dollars in merit funding that mainly focus on a student's involvement. Therefore, grades, scores, and other factors such as financial need or ethnicity, for example, are secondary at most.

Everyone Can Serve

One of the best ways to build your Robust Resume is by becoming a social entrepreneur. A social entrepreneur is defined as one who creates and implements a project involving something for which they are passionate. Clients of Scholarship Solutions, as young as age three, have turned their passion projects into social entrepreneurship. For examples, please visit the websites of these incredible young social entrepreneurs!

- **Heroes and Hearts: heroesandhearts.org**
- **Books and Ballet: booksandballet.com**
- **Klothes 4 Kids: klothes4kidslv.org**
- **Cool and Dope: coolanddope.com**

Because of their commitments to community and civic engagement, these scholars have secured 1000s of dollars in grants, scholarships, awards, and more. So, pursue your passion and win big!

The Three C's

Maybe starting a non-profit seems a bit daunting, especially as a toddler! Please do not worry; you can support your passion by volunteering for local, national, or international organizations. When it comes to community service, think about things you enjoy. Are you an animal lover? Do you enjoy working with plants? Are you someone who likes kids, or maybe you enjoy museums. There are an endless number of places and ways you can volunteer and give back. Consequently, these types of activities and so many more will build your Robust Resume. Now, I do need to caution you, you should not try and do everything. In fact, the way to win at the scholarship game in relation to building a Robust Resume is:

- **Creativity**
- **Consistency**
- **Community**

Creativity: Look for volunteer opportunities that are unique. I have loved when my Scholarship Solutions' clients have volunteered with therapy horses, spent their time giving back at the Social Justice or Law Enforcement Museums, or befriended young teens with Down Syndrome. Participating in creative volunteer activities will help build your Robust Resume.

Consistency: Seemingly, since I am saying have a Robust Resume, you may be thinking, "I need to volunteer at a bunch of different places!" However, this is not the best approach. Consequently, students should have two different organizations that can count on their consistent participation. The most incredible volunteer pattern is giving back to two organizations two hours per month. So, that is a total of four hours of monthly service learning. Maintaining a consistent volunteer esthetic is imperative for merit scholarships.

Community: Giving back to your place of worship, school, or family business can unequivocally curate scholarships. A few things I love about helping with these types of community groups are 1) You can traditionally start volunteering very young. One of my youngest clients started volunteering at his church when he was approximately nine months old. Now as an early elementary student, he is still very involved with supporting his church with his time. He will have a long history of giving back to his community because of the opportunities through his church. 2) These community groups normally have an array of unique opportunities. For example, for a place of worship you may be a member of the choir, the parking lot team, the children's ministry and more. At school you can be the hall monitor, a student tutor, a volunteer groundskeeper, or the manager of the student store. If you are volunteering for the family business, you may be the cashier, server, or front desk clerk. As a result, the diversity of service learning options expands your resume, filling it with so many skills while also providing you with essay material where you can discuss working with people from various ages, ethnic groups, and other phenomenal character traits.

Now, you may be saying, "Scholarship Doctor, thank you for providing me with the volunteer prescription," but at the same time asking, "Why is volunteering so important to earning scholarships?" Well, many times scholarship funders are looking for well-rounded students. Therefore, they want to see that a student can successfully balance school, extra-curricular activities, and community service. Once someone has built their resume, they will be attractive to scholarship funders, which will bring big rewards in the form of scholarship dollars. Begin volunteering in pre-school and never stop giving back to your local community and beyond.

Dial 211

I have provided you with examples of successful community service change agents as well as samples of places where you can give back. However, I also want to give you a few important resources to help you navigate successfully through the volunteer processes. First, **Dial 211** for information about volunteer opportunities. If you are in the United States, this phone number works the exact same way as 911, 411, 611, and others. It is a toll-free number that provides access to social service organizations and assistance in your community. Call them, let them know about the area(s) you are interested in volunteering and they will provide a list of places that may fit your needs. Second, **visit www.volunteermatch.org**. This website has listings of organizations within a five-mile radius of your home and beyond. You can also search for virtual/at-home volunteer opportunities. You are needed! Use these important resources to help launch your volunteer career. Finally, here are a few more examples of unique volunteer options:

Urban Garden Assistant

Beach Cleanup Volunteer

Memory Care Facility Helper

Knit Hats, Gloves, and Scarves for Dialysis Patients

Throw Birthday Parties for Kids Experiencing Homelessness

Babysit Puppies and Kittens on Adoption Day

Remember, passion projects and entrepreneurial endeavors help to set you apart from others when competing for scholarships and equate to "dollars for scholars." Start volunteering and building your Robust Resume, today.

"She assisted me in pursuing my dreams as a **Master's** level student."

- Graduate Scholar

NOW LET'S FILL THE PRESCRIPTION

☐ I have contacted 211.

☐ I have visited volunteermatch.org.

Top 5 Things I Enjoy:

1. ____________________
2. ____________________
3. ____________________
4. ____________________
5. ____________________

Top 5 Places I Want to Serve:

1. ____________________
2. ____________________
3. ____________________
4. ____________________
5. ____________________

Volunteer Tracker-Write Your Volunteer Details

Organization Name/Duties/Hours:

1. ______________________________

____

2. ______________________________

____

3. ______________________________

____

4. ______________________________

____

Find this tracker in
Chapter 7: Funding Facts, Final Thoughts & Forms
on page 127

NOW LET'S APPLY WHAT WE LEARNED

I will make the following changes:

1. ____

2. ____

3. ____

THE PROGRESS SO FAR

The changes I made gave me these results:

1. ______________________________

____

____

2. ______________________________

____

____

3. ______________________________

____

____

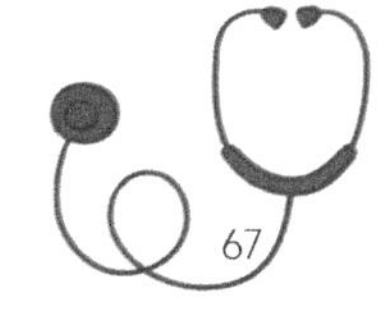

"Don't com-
pare yourself
to others. You
were made to
order."

- Scholarship Doctor

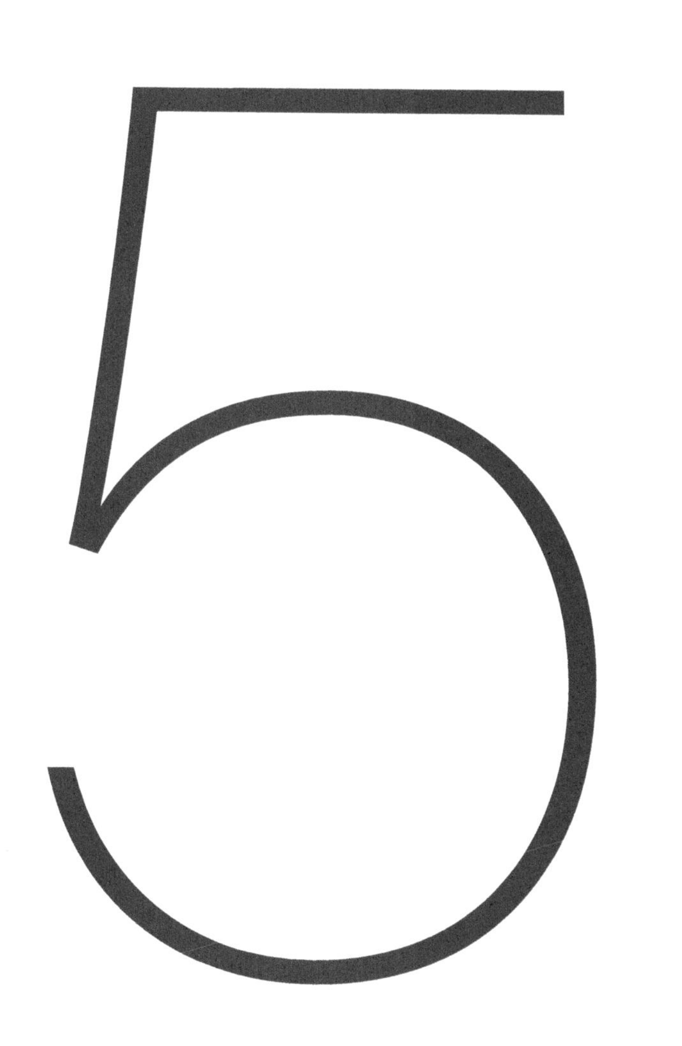

Step Five: EXCELLENT **EXTRACURRICULAR ACTIVITIES**

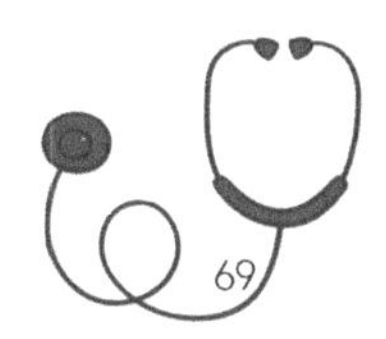

Scholarship Club

The Ping Pong Club, Corndog Eating Club, Waffle Making Club, Tropical Fish Owners Club, Sports Broadcasting Club, Pi (3.14) Club, or Create Your Own Club. These are just a few examples of uniquely unusual clubs and organizations that when you join, belong to, or start can turn into big scholarship dollars. Remember last chapter when we discussed R and R? Well, another important contributor to your Robust Resume is extra-curricular activities in which you are involved both inside and outside of school.

Extracurricular activities are defined as participation in areas, arenas, actions, and activities outside of your required schoolwork/classwork. At the beginning of this chapter, I listed clubs that you may have never heard of or knew about but, believe it or not, they are all legitimate. Because of the uniqueness of these example clubs, I have students who were able to successfully write about their participation in a scholarship essay which in turn helped them to secure 1000s of dollars in scholarships for college.

One of my Scholarship Solutions clients started the Ping Pong Club at their high school. They had always enjoyed the game and thought others may like to play as well. To start a club at their school, they needed three students and that is just what they got, they and two other students who were interested in the game. Excitedly, during every lunch period they would eat and play ping pong. Additionally, they appointed officers: President, Vice President, and Secretary/Treasurer. Finally, they sponsored regular give-back activities where all three members were gaining volunteer hours. This ingenious club did so many things for my student, including:

- **Promoted a healthy lifestyle through exercise and sport**
- **Showed leadership by being the founder and president of a unique club**
- **Generated strong relationships and bonds with friends**
- **Motivated other students to participate in extra-curricular activities and community service**
- **Demonstrated a spirit of community by giving back and serving**

Honestly, this club idea sort of started out as a running joke, but in the end helped my student to earn 1000s of dollars in merit-based scholarships and to attend college debt free.

Extracurricular activities should be approached in the same manner as community service. As a result, you should participate in two extracurricular actives per month and stay consistent with that involvement throughout your entire educational journey. So, for example, if you become a member of the Pi Club in ninth grade, attend the monthly meetings, participate in the activities being hosted by the club, and take advantage of leadership opportunities as they become available.

Scholarship funders are seeking students who have shown consistency, longevity, and commitment. Consequently, if you start archery as a 10th grader, no matter how difficult the sport becomes, do not quit; continue at least until you graduate high school. Therefore, you can discuss the challenges, what you have learned, the people you have met, the leadership roles you secured, or the importance of being involved in the group. These are just a few examples of what can be shared in a scholarship or college interview, application, or essay. So continue to build your Robust Resume through regular – long term involvement in a club or organization.

What About Scouts?

We have discussed some pretty unique extracurricular clubs and activities, things like the Corndog Eating Club, Archery, Pi Club and more. However, you may be saying, "But I have been a Scout since I was in elementary school. Does that "count"? The answer is Yes! Absolutely! If you are a member of Girl or Boy Scouts, have been involved with 4-H, participated in Future Business Leaders of America, are an officer with the Black Student Union, a member of Fellowship of Christian Athletes, or have been inducted in National Junior Honor Society, it is all important, worthy, builds your Robust Resume, and yes, "counts". Any and all extra-curricular activities, whether creative and unique or well-established and well-known, are all rewarding contributors to your Robust Resume and can lead to Robust Rewards in the scholarship world.

The Secret Sauce

Although creative extracurricular activities can score big points for you when applying for scholarships, as explained, there are plenty of well-established organizations that will give you a big boost, too. What is most important to the scholarship process is being involved and doing more than attending school, classes, academic seminars or sessions, etc. Moreover, there is a secret sauce to help further increase your chances of winning scholarship dollars and/or being accepted to your dream college. The secret has been mentioned briefly throughout the book, but in this section, we will address it directly. The way Scholarship Solutions clients have secured millions of dollars in scholarship funding is through their commitment to leadership.

Scholarship and college applications are very interested in what you have done for your community. They want you to discuss your fun extra-curricular activities but, there will always be space for you to explain how you were the founder, creator, coordinator, president, sergeant of arms, chairperson, junior senator, captain, choreographer, chaplain, representative, leader, etc. for a group, club, or organization that you either started or joined.

Leadership positions show a scholarship funder or admission officer that you are willing to do more than what is required, to go beyond the bare minimum, and that you are not afraid of hardwork. Your leadership position can demonstrate that you are a team player, your ability to motivate others, to resolve conflict, speak with authority, sportsmanship, and so much more. In fact, in this section of the workbook, please take a few minutes and list some of the skills and attributes you are currently demonstrating as a leader.

Taking on leadership roles sets you apart from the applicant who is “just” a member. Your willingness to step-up immediately gives a scholarship judge the sense that you are sacrificial with your time and energy, and that as a leader you are a sojourner for your cause or club. A popular scholarship essay question asks: **What does leadership mean to you?** When you have been in the role of a leader, you can easily answer about the challenges and wins you have experienced. Additionally, you can give a strong definition of leadership. Contrarily, when you have not put yourself out there to "Win or Learn" in regard to running for office against a friend, having to clock the fastest speed, or perhaps answer a question on the spot during an on-stage pageant interview, you may not be able to adequately address how you have learned or grown through your experiences as a leader. So, go for it! Do not be afraid to run for office or try out for the captain position. Unequivocally, leadership leads to scholarships.

This chapter primarily discussed extracurricular activities that someone may participate in through their school or university. However, there are tons of opportunities to take part in community-based groups as well. Therefore, being a member of a fencing league, or sitting on the board of a chamber of commerce, perhaps you coach or referee for a sports league for athletes with developmental challenges, or you are a member of a trial by peers cohort, these types of amazing activities add to your resume just like a school-based club. Also, participating in national civic groups like the NAACP, American Heart Association, Cooperative Extension, The Elks Lodge/Foundation, or the VFW is just as credible (See **Chapter 8** for scholarship details). Again, regardless if you have created your own organization or joined a national or international club, stay involved, do not quit, go for a leadership position, and apply for scholarships that will reward you for your Robust Resume!

Here are a few more examples of extracurricular activities:

National/International Organizations

- **Golden Key International Honour Society**
- **Debbie's Dream Foundation School Club**
- **International Thespian Society**
- **Sororities and Fraternities**
- **National Urban League**
- **National Honor Society**
- **National Beta Club**
- **Jack and Jill**
- **Skills USA**
- **HOSA**

School-Based Clubs/Organizations

- **Black or Latinx Student Union**
- **International Student Club**
- **Cake Baking Club**
- **Board Game Club**
- **Student Council**
- **Science Club**
- **Anime Club**
- **Math Club**
- **Robotics**

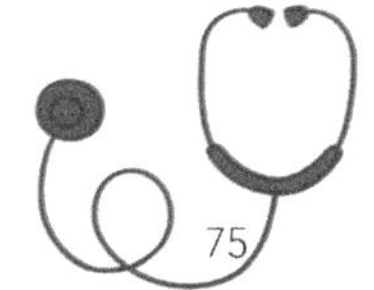

Committees

- Communications Committee
- Green School Committee
- Homecoming Committee
- Technology Committee
- Fundraising Committee
- Multicultural Committee
- Yearbook Committee
- Birthday Committee
- Library Committee
- Prom Committee

Sports

- Swimming
- Basketball
- Volleyball
- Lacrosse
- Softball
- Bowling
- Rowing
- Cheer
- Tennis
- Soccer

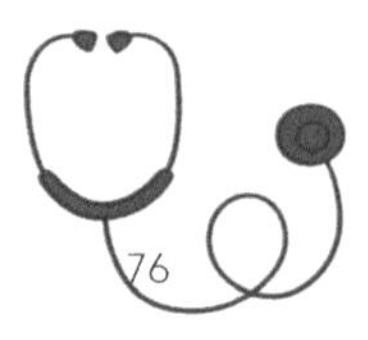

Music

- **Color Guard**
- **Show Choir**
- **Ensemble**
- **Orchestra**
- **Chamber**
- **Chorale**
- **Chorus**
- **Opera**
- **Dance**
- **Band**

"We started with Dr. Rhee in **Elementary School.**"

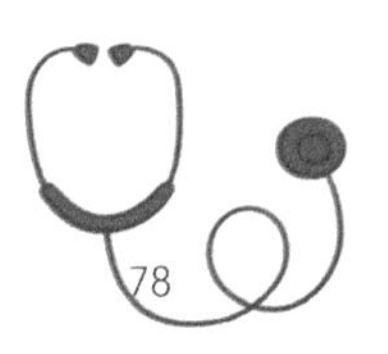

- Early Starter Parent

"My son won his first **$100 award** in 4th grade!"

- Saving For College

NOW LET'S FILL THE PRESCRIPTION

☐ I have joined a club at my school or in my community.

☐ I have started a club at my school or in my community.

Top 5 Activities I Enjoy:

1. ______________________

2. ______________________

3. ______________________

4. ______________________

5. ______________________

Top 5 Clubs I Want to Start/Join at School or in my Community:

1. ______________________

2. ______________________

3. ______________________

4. ______________________

5. ______________________

Extracurricular Activities Tracker-Write Your Activity Details

Organization Name/Office Held/Leadership Status/Dates/Hours:

1. ____

____

2. ____

____

3. ____

____

4. ____

____

Find this tracker in
Chapter 7: Funding Facts, Final Thoughts & Forms
on page 137

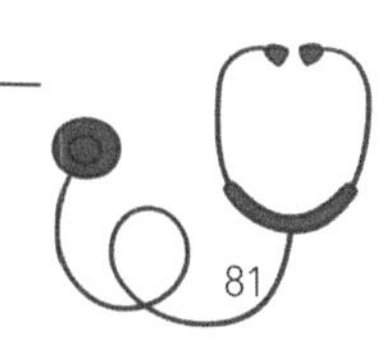

NOW LET'S APPLY WHAT WE LEARNED

I will make the following changes:

1. ______________________________

____

____

2. ______________________________

____

____

3. ______________________________

____

____

THE PROGRESS SO FAR

The changes I made gave me these results:

1.

2.

3.

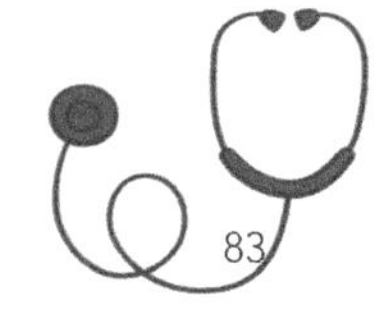

"Be you! Only you can do that!"

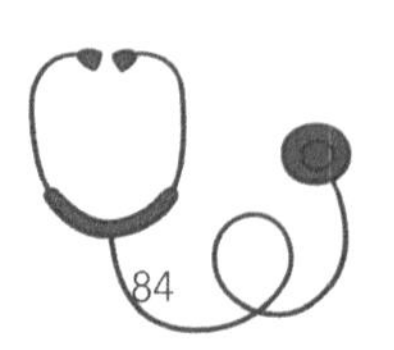

- Scholarship Doctor

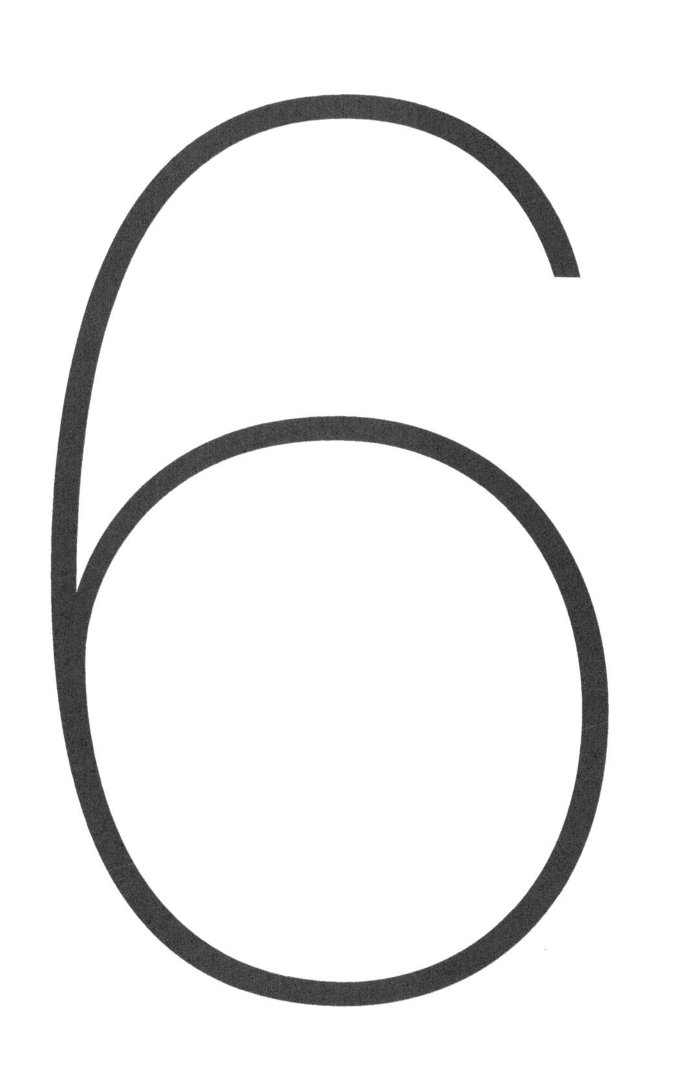

Chapter Six: **Internships, Majors, Camps & Careers**

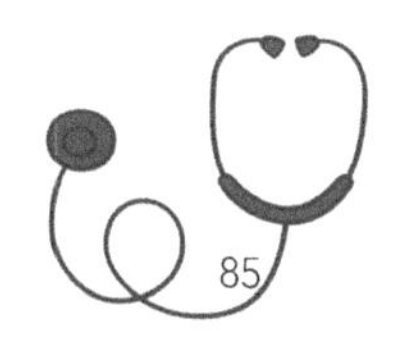

Science Equals Scholarships

Think **SMART**, take a **STEM**, feel the **STEAM**! This is one of the most important slogans with Scholarships Solutions. Why? Because when students consider fields associated with the acronyms **SMART, STEM, STEAM,** you can practically write your own ticket to debt freedom. What are **SMART, STEM, and STEAM** fields? They are internships, majors, and professions in science and math. Specifically, they are defined as:

SMART: Science, Math, Agriculture, Research, and Technology

STEM: Science, Technology, Engineering, and Math

STEAM: Science, Technology, Engineering Agriculture, and Math

Choosing these majors and careers can garner huge scholarship dollars. Science and math activities and options are available for all age groups. There are opportunities for young children to participate in camps, attend pre-Kindergarten programs, schools, and summer events all connected to **SMART/STEM/STEAM**. Additionally, these same possibilities are available beyond the nursery and elementary stages, allowing students to participate in **STEM** activities, academic programs, internships, and more during middle and high school, as well as in college and careers. Amazingly, did you know the majors associated with **STEM**, many times, require a 4-year degree at most? Therefore, in order to start a successful career in **STEM**, it only requires a bachelor's degree and in some instances an associate's degree, certification, and/or special training. Incredibly, when you are focused on **SMART/STEM/STEAM** you can earn lots of scholarships, you do not have to invest a lot of time or money in your education, and these professions allow you to have a long-standing and financially-rewarding career.

You may be wondering, why are the **STEM** fields so appealing to scholarship funders and college admissions counselors? One reason is because these areas are very underrepresented. However, there are so many available jobs and careers connected to these disciplines. As a result, since people are needed to fill positions available in **Science, Math, Engineering, Research, Agriculture, and Technology,** it causes students to be more desirable and more likely to earn financial awards and entrance into top colleges! Therefore, think **SMART** and you will earn BIG dollars for college.

So, to reiterate, in addition to going college and selecting majors in the areas of **SMART, STEM, STEAM,** you should apply regularly to academic and leadership camps and internships with **STEM** themes. You should also apply for scholarships and study abroad programs that focus on these subjects and disciplines. Finally, become a professional within the **SMART/STEM/STEAM** arena. You will find yourself in a fulfilling, strong income-producing field that can lead to many other professional opportunities outside of **STEM**.

<u>Science Disciplines</u>

1. **Biology**
2. **Chemistry**
3. **Physics**
4. **Meteorology**
5. **Paleontology**

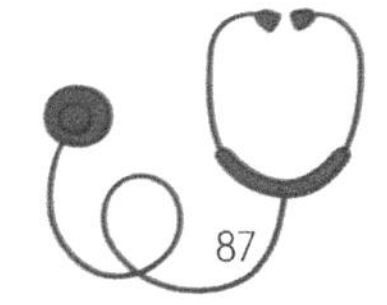

6. **Aeronautics**
7. **Zoology**
8. **Biochemistry**
9. **Astronomy**
10. **Neuroscience**

<u>Math Disciplines</u>

1. **Actuary**
2. **Statistician**
3. **Economist**
4. **Analyst**
5. **Accountant**
6. **Cryptographer**
7. **Biostatistician**
8. **Logician**
9. **Teacher/Professor**
10. **Stockbroker**

<u>Agricultural Disciplines</u>

1. **Agronomy**
2. **Animal Science**
3. **Environmental Science**
4. **Horticulture**
5. **Equine Science**
6. **Forestry**

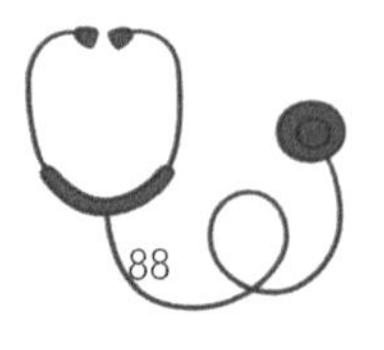

7. **Agricultural Business**
8. **Nutrition**
9. **Fashion Design & Textiles**
10. **Sustainable Agriculture**

<u>Research Disciplines</u>

1. **Brain Science**
2. **Epidemiology**
3. **Medical Laboratory Science**
4. **Library and Information Science**
5. **Geography**
6. **Sports Science**
7. **Hematology**
8. **Psychopharmacology**
9. **Computer Research Science**
10. **Immunology**

<u>Technology Disciplines</u>

1. **Biotechnology**
2. **Cyber and Cloud Security**
3. **Hardware and Software Development**
4. **Artificial Intelligence**
5. **Computer Science**
6. **Coding and App Development**
7. **Data Management**

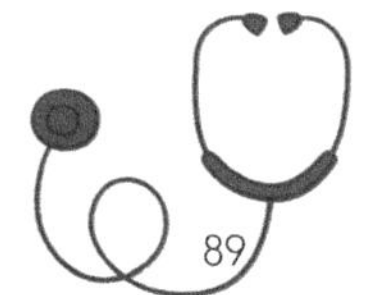

8. **Computer Information Systems**
9. **Network Administration**
10. **Management Information Systems**

<u>Engineering Disciplines</u>

1. **Agricultural Engineer**
2. **Petroleum Engineer**
3. **Biomedical Engineer**
4. **Civil Engineer**
5. **Automotive Engineer**
6. **Mining Engineer**
7. **Chemical Engineer**
8. **Marine Engineer**
9. **Data Engineer**
10. **Environmental Engineer**

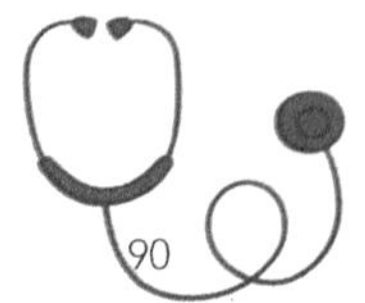

"Working with the Scholarship Doctor trained me for my future career & school."

- Highly Motivated Scholar

NOW LET'S FILL THE PRESCRIPTION

☐ I have researched "**SMART**" fields.

My top 5 **SMART** fields:

1. ____________________
2. ____________________
3. ____________________
4. ____________________
5. ____________________

☐ I have researched "**STEM**" fields.

My top 5 **STEM** fields:

1. ____________________
2. ____________________
3. ____________________
4. ____________________
5. ____________________

☐ I have researched "**STEAM**" fields.

My top 5 **STEAM** fields:

1. ______________________
2. ______________________
3. ______________________
4. ______________________
5. ______________________

My top 5 colleges with my favorite **SMART/STEM/STEAM** majors:

1. ____
2. ____
3. ____
4. ____
5. ____

My top 5 colleges **SMART/STEM/STEAM** Scholarships & Requirements:

1. ______________________________

____

2. ______________________________

____

3. ______________________________

____

4. ______________________________

____

5. ______________________________

____

Summer Camp/Internship Tracker-Write Your Camp/Internship Details

Organization Name/Requirements/Camp Theme/Dates/Cost or Credits Received/Duties/Leadership Roles:

1. ______________________________

____

2. ______________________________

____

3. ______________________________

____

Find this tracker in
Chapter 7: Funding Facts, Final Thoughts & Forms
on page 147

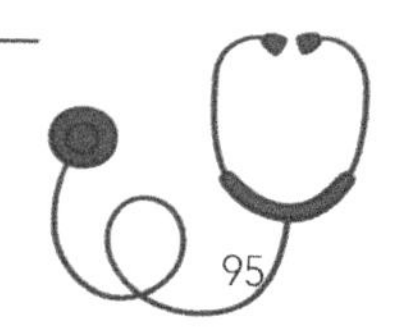

NOW LET'S APPLY WHAT WE LEARNED

I will make the following changes:

1. ______________________________

____

____

2. ______________________________

____

____

3. ______________________________

____

____

THE PROGRESS SO FAR

The changes I made gave me these results:

1. ____________________

2. ____________________

3. ____________________

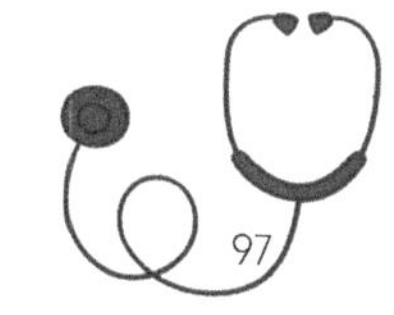

"Don't de-
lay, apply for
scholarships
today!"

- Scholarship Doctor

Chapter Seven: **Funding Facts, Final Thoughts & Forms**

Funding and Finances

Thus far, you have learned about the five easy steps needed to win big at the scholarship game. These steps are:

1. **Earn** Good **Grades.**
2. **Have a** Good **Class Rank.**
3. **Have** Good **Test Scores.**
4. **Have EXCELLENT Volunteer History.**
5. **Have EXCELLENT Extracurricular Activities.**

You have also learned that Leadership = Scholarships, and the importance of choosing the right major and career, which should be in the **STEAM** fields of Science, Technology, Engineering, Agriculture and Math.

Although these prescriptions are imperative in regard to academic and merit-based funding, there are other funding methods that can be used to attend college as well. In this chapter, we will discuss the different types of scholarship categories, as well as provide information regarding funding available from different states in the U.S., the FAFSA application, which is U.S. federal aid, and the CSS Profile, nonfederal financial aid.

Scholarships

During the Myths and Truths section and throughout various chapters we have talked about scholarship categories a bit, but now we will do a deep dive by defining what a scholarship is and what types are available.

First, a scholarship is free money from a college or business that does not have to be repaid. There are scholarships for all kinds of traits associated with a student so let us explore these types now.

If you recall, there are **merit scholarships,** which primarily take into account (or, primarily look at) your Robust Resume. Therefore, they want to know what you have done for your community, what you have been involved in over time, and what leadership positions you have secured.

There are also **music scholarships.** You can earn a scholarship from a college by being a member of the marching band or show choir for example. Additionally, there are scholarships available because you play a particular instrument or because you have been involved in a music-based organization either in school or your community.

There are **athletic scholarships** available to students who play any number of team or individualized sports. Colleges and universities provide scholarships for all types of sports, not just the "big" ones like baseball, basketball, volleyball, soccer, or football. For example, you can also earn scholarships for cheer, fencing, golf, tennis, rowing, diving, gymnastics, and so much more. However, there are also funds available outside of a college or university where you can win a scholarship for being an athlete in general or because of a specified sport in which you play.

There are **art scholarships,** too. Although art scholarships can be a bit more difficult to come by than other types of scholarships, they surely exist. This is especially true for students who are in lower grades. They have the opportunity to participate in coloring and drawing contests. However, undergraduate and graduate students who may be studying fine arts can apply for scholarships and fellowships in art.

Next are **academic scholarships,** and as mentioned in Step 1, you want a 3.8 GPA, minimally, when competing for academic scholarships. The reality is, if you want to earn scholarships based on your transcript, the expectation is perfect grades or really close to it. So for this type of scholarship, it is all about the A and A grades.

Scholarships based on **financial need** are looking at families who make less than $50,000 per year. Traditionally, scholarships will signify *"need-based scholarship"* or *"must show financial need."* With these statements, they are looking to see if you show a family income of less than $50,000.

Miscellaneous Components are scholarships connected to a myriad of different topics such as:

- **Age**
- **Ability**
- **Military**
- **Gender**
- **Hobbies**
- **Religion**
- **Where You Live**
- **College Type**
- **Ethnicity**
- **What High School You Attended**

As you can see, there are scholarships for everyone. So, "don't delay, apply for scholarships today!"

States Give Scholarships

In the U.S., there are lots of states that celebrate students who choose to attend college in the state in which they reside. Therefore, "staying home" or close to home for college/university and produce a huge funding award in regard to scholarships. Additionally, there is state-based financial aid and/or grant (free money) funds for students who decide to stay in their home state for school. Finally, there are scholarships and reduced tuition agreements among states in the same region. For example, if you live in Nevada, you can attend college in California and a number of other regional institutions for a discounted rate. Here are some examples of states that have scholarships, grants, and financial aid for their residents.

State Scholarship Programs

Nevada - Millennium Scholarship

Kentucky - Kentucky Educational Excellence

Georgia - Hope Scholarship

Missouri - Bright Flight Program

South Carolina - Legislative Incentive for Future Excellence (LIFE)

State Grant Programs

California - CAL Grant

Texas - Toward Excellence, Access, and Success Grant Program (TEXAS Grant)

Vermont - Vermont Grant

Minnesota - Minnesota Grant

Oregon - Oregon Promise Grant

State Financial Aid and Scholarship Programs

- **Colorado**
- **Delaware**
- **Maryland**
- **Florida**
- **Illinois**

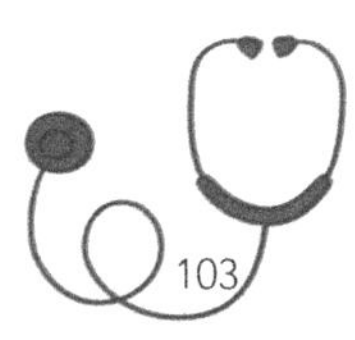

FAFSA

The Free Application for Federal Student Aid, FAFSA, is available to all eligible students in October of each year. Graduating high school seniors, undergraduate students, and graduate/professional students who are United States citizens and residents can apply for federal financial aid. The application process should occur on a yearly basis and whenever possible, apply October 1, when the application opens. Applying early helps to assure that your application is one the first to be processed and could provide you with the greatest amount of funding for which you are eligible.

Additionally, every college campus has a financial aid office. Therefore, they are the coordinators of any funding you may receive for college. In general, there are different federal financial sources. They are:

Federal Loans:

Subsidized Loan - This loan is interest free while you are a student. So, as long as you pay back what you borrow, before you graduate college, there is no interest. However, if you do not pay the loan back by graduation (there is a six-month grace period after you receive your degree) all of the interest that has been in deferment, as well as the original loan amount, is yours to pay.

Unsubsidized Loan - This student loan begins to accrue interest immediately. However, your payments, not the interest, are deferred, (there is a six-month grace period after you receive your degree) until you graduate college.

Parent Loans - These loans work like your mortgage, car payments, credit cards, or other installment plans. Therefore, there is no grace period with this type of loan. Also, please understand the debt you accrue on a parent loan is your debt. It does not belong to your student/child at any time, including once they have received their degree.

Graduate Loans: These loans are available to students who are studying for graduate or professional degrees. The payments for these loans can be deferred until after graduation.

Federal Grants: Grants are funds that do not have to be repaid. Traditionally, grant funds range from $200 - $6,500 a year. There are several federal grant programs. Firstly, there is the Pell Grant. Pell funds are provided to undergraduate students who show financial need. Secondly, there is the TEACH - Teacher Education Assistance for College and Higher Education Grant. This grant is up to $4,000 and is available to undergraduate students as well as graduate students who are pursuing degrees in K - 12 education.

Federal Work Study: Federal Work-Study is a part-time job providing undergraduate and graduate students the opportunity to earn money to help pay educational expenses. With work study, students should never work more than eight hours in one day or 20 hours in one week, other than at times when classes are not in session, full-time work is allowable during those breaks.

Truly, FAFSA helps students and families supplement the costs of higher education, yet too many people fail to apply for financial aid, thinking that in some way they are not qualified for funding. However, if you are eligible for federal funding, please apply. Your FAFSA documents are an important part of the scholarship process. So do not disqualify yourself from scholarships or federal funding options by eliminating the FAFSA application. To apply for financial aid, go to: **www.fafsa.gov.**

CSS Profile

The College Scholarship Service Profile - CSS Profile is an application that over 200 colleges, like Alabama A&M University, Carnegie Mellon University, George Washington University, Texas Christian University, and Saint Louis University, just to name a few, use to provide students with financial aid directly from the college(s). CSS can be a resource to provide funding to students who are U.S, citizens or those from other parts or the world. More information regarding this online form can be found here: **cssprofile.org**

Final Thoughts

Well everyone, that is it! You have a winning prescription and are equipped to be highly successful with your scholarship and college processes! Thank you for giving me the opportunity to take this debt-free degree journey with you.Now remember, to win at the scholarship game – you must apply. If you need or want additional assistance, we would love to work with you! If you did not know, we have a thriving monthly scholarship membership. We also offer individual VIP client services and we would love to speak at your church, community-based organization, school, library, college/university, fraternity/sorority, or other groups. For more information regarding the above, as well as our virtual ACT/SAT classes, other books, services, and more, please visit our website www.myscholarshipsolutions.com. We would also love for you be a part of our social media communities, where we can be found @scholarshipdr. I pray all of your scholarship dreams come true. I believe in you and know you CAN and ARE accomplishing your goals and soaring to amazing heights!

- Rhea, The Scholarship Doctor

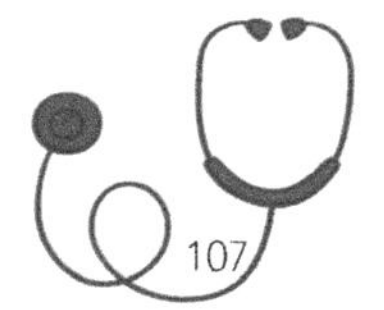

"...scholarship membership is a **community**, my child and I needed."

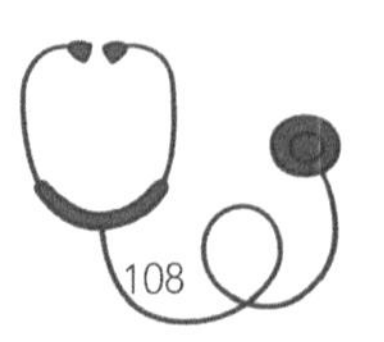

- Membership Parent

"The information shared in the scholarship membership is gold."

\- Membership Parent

NOW LET'S FILL THE PRESCRIPTION

☐ I have researched my state's scholarship program.

Top 5 Funding Programs in my state:

1. ____________________

4. ____________________

2. ____________________

5. ____________________

3. ____________________

☐ I have researched federal & local funding for my college & major.

Top 5 Federal, Local, College, & Major Funding Sources:

1. ____________________

4. ____________________

2. ____________________

5. ____________________

3. ____________________

☐ I have researched federal grants.

My top 5 Federal Grants:

1. ______________________

4. ______________________

2. ______________________

5. ______________________

3. ______________________

My top 5 funding programs based on my college, major, & state:

1. ____

2. ____

3. ____

4. ____

5. ____

NOW LET'S APPLY WHAT WE LEARNED

I will make the following changes:

1. ______________________________

____

____

2. ______________________________

____

____

3. ______________________________

____

____

THE PROGRESS SO FAR

The changes I made gave me these results:

1. ____

2. ____

3. ____

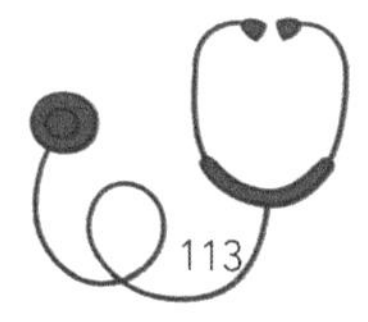

NOW LET'S FILL THE PRESCRIPTION

Full Name: ______________________________

Complete Address: ______________________________

____

Phone: ______________________________

Email Address: ______________________________

Classification: ______________

Date of Graduation: ______________

Unweighted GPA: ______________

Weighted GPA: ______________

This Year's Educational Goal: ______________________________

Scholarship Builder Form

Explain what you want to do, i.e. apply for a scholarship, apply to college, apply for an internship, etc. (this is your objective):

____

____

____

____

List any organizations, clubs, sports teams, choirs, bands, theatrical groups, etc. that you have been a member. Include the number of years, dates, positions, and/or any leadership roles:

____

____

____

Scholarship Builder Form

List any volunteer projects in which you have participated. Please include years/dates:

____

____

____

____

List awards, certificates, prizes, and/or contests that you have won. Include the year/date of when they were earned:

____

____

____

Scholarship Tracker-Write Your Scholarship Details

Organization Name/Requirements (Grades/Test Scores/Volunteer Experience) Amount/Transcript or Letters of Recommendation/Due Date:

1. ______________________________

____

2. ______________________________

____

3. ______________________________

____

4. ______________________________

____

Scholarship Tracker:

Organization Name/Requirements (Grades/Test Scores/Volunteer Experience) Amount/Transcript or Letters of Recommendation/Due Date:

1. ____

____

2. ____

____

3. ____

____

4. ____

____

Scholarship Tracker:

Organization Name/Requirements (Grades/Test Scores/Volunteer Experience) Amount/Transcript or Letters of Recommendation/Due Date:

1. ______________________________

____

2. ______________________________

____

3. ______________________________

____

4. ______________________________

____

Scholarship Tracker:

Organization Name/Requirements (Grades/Test Scores/Volunteer Experience) Amount/Transcript or Letters of Recommendation/Due Date:

1. ____

____

2. ____

____

3. ____

____

4. ____

____

Scholarship Tracker:

Organization Name/Requirements (Grades/Test Scores/Volunteer Experience) Amount/Transcript or Letters of Recommendation/Due Date:

1. ____

____

2. ____

____

3. ____

____

4. ____

____

Scholarship Tracker:

Organization Name/Requirements (Grades/Test Scores/Volunteer Experience) Amount/Transcript or Letters of Recommendation/Due Date:

1. ______________________________

____

2. ______________________________

____

3. ______________________________

____

4. ______________________________

____

Scholarship Tracker:

Organization Name/Requirements (Grades/Test Scores/Volunteer Experience) Amount/Transcript or Letters of Recommendation/Due Date:

1. ____

   ____

2. ____

   ____

3. ____

   ____

4. ____

   ____

Scholarship Tracker:

Organization Name/Requirements (Grades/Test Scores/Volunteer Experience) Amount/Transcript or Letters of Recommendation/Due Date:

1. ______________________________

____

2. ______________________________

____

3. ______________________________

____

4. ______________________________

____

Scholarship Tracker:

Organization Name/Requirements (Grades/Test Scores/Volunteer Experience) Amount/Transcript or Letters of Recommendation/Due Date:

1. ____

____

2. ____

____

3. ____

____

4. ____

____

Scholarship Tracker:

Organization Name/Requirements (Grades/Test Scores/Volunteer Experience) Amount/Transcript or Letters of Recommendation/Due Date:

1. ______________________________

____

2. ______________________________

____

3. ______________________________

____

4. ______________________________

____

Volunteer Tracker-Write Your Volunteer Details

Organization Name/Duties/Hours:

1. ______________________________

____

2. ______________________________

____

3. ______________________________

____

4. ______________________________

____

Volunteer Tracker:

Organization Name/Duties/Hours:

1. ______________________________

____

2. ______________________________

____

3. ______________________________

____

4. ______________________________

____

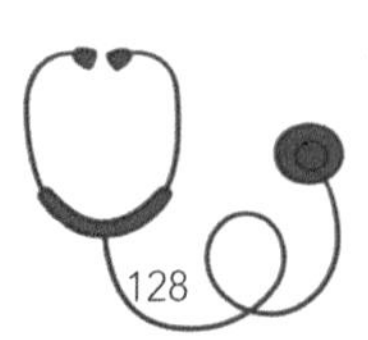

Volunteer Tracker:

Organization Name/Duties/Hours:

1. ____

____

2. ____

____

3. ____

____

4. ____

____

Volunteer Tracker:

Organization Name/Duties/Hours:

1. ______________________________

____

2. ______________________________

____

3. ______________________________

____

4. ______________________________

____

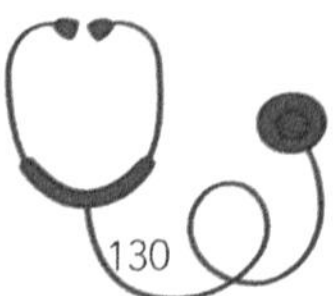

Volunteer Tracker:

Organization Name/Duties/Hours:

1. ______________________________

____

2. ______________________________

____

3. ______________________________

____

4. ______________________________

____

Volunteer Tracker:

Organization Name/Duties/Hours:

1. ______________________________

____

2. ______________________________

____

3. ______________________________

____

4. ______________________________

____

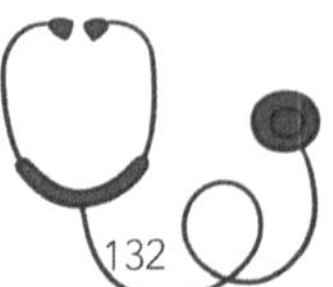

Volunteer Tracker:

Organization Name/Duties/Hours:

1. ______________________________

____

2. ______________________________

____

3. ______________________________

____

4. ______________________________

____

Volunteer Tracker:

Organization Name/Duties/Hours:

1. ____

____

2. ____

____

3. ____

____

4. ____

____

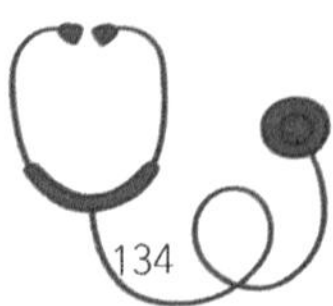

Volunteer Tracker:

Organization Name/Duties/Hours:

1. ______________________________

____

2. ______________________________

____

3. ______________________________

____

4. ______________________________

____

Volunteer Tracker:

Organization Name/Duties/Hours:

1. ______________________________

____

2. ______________________________

____

3. ______________________________

____

4. ______________________________

____

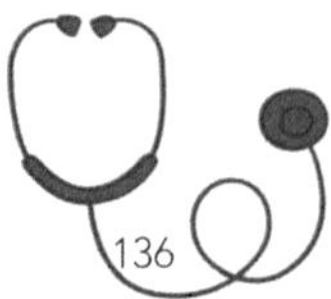

Extracurricular Activities Tracker-Write Your Activity Details

Organization Name/Office Held/Leadership Status/Dates/Hours:

1. ____

____

2. ____

____

3. ____

____

4. ____

____

Extracurricular Activities Tracker:

Organization Name/Office Held/Leadership Status/Dates/Hours:

1. ____

   ____

2. ____

   ____

3. ____

   ____

4. ____

   ____

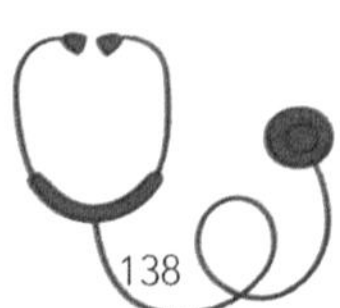

Extracurricular Activities Tracker:

Organization Name/Office Held/Leadership Status/Dates/Hours:

1. ____

____

2. ____

____

3. ____

____

4. ____

____

Extracurricular Activities Tracker:

Organization Name/Office Held/Leadership Status/Dates/Hours:

1. ______________________________

____

2. ______________________________

____

3. ______________________________

____

4. ______________________________

____

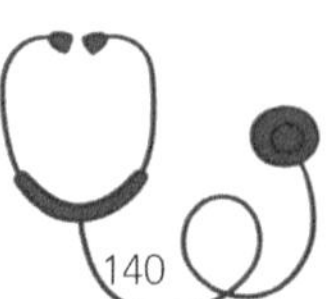

Extracurricular Activities Tracker:

Organization Name/Office Held/Leadership Status/Dates/Hours:

1. ____

____

2. ____

____

3. ____

____

4. ____

____

Extracurricular Activities Tracker:

Organization Name/Office Held/Leadership Status/Dates/Hours:

1. ______________________________

____

2. ______________________________

____

3. ______________________________

____

4. ______________________________

____

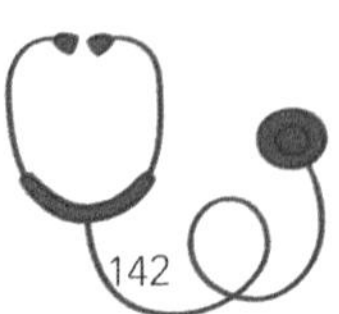

Extracurricular Activities Tracker:

Organization Name/Office Held/Leadership Status/Dates/Hours:

1. ______________________________

____

2. ______________________________

____

3. ______________________________

____

4. ______________________________

____

Extracurricular Activities Tracker:

Organization Name/Office Held/Leadership Status/Dates/Hours:

1. ______________________________

____

2. ______________________________

____

3. ______________________________

____

4. ______________________________

____

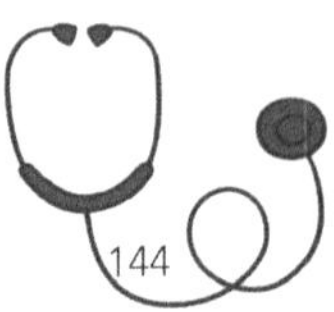

Extracurricular Activities Tracker:

Organization Name/Office Held/Leadership Status/Dates/Hours:

1. ____

   ____

2. ____

   ____

3. ____

   ____

4. ____

   ____

Extracurricular Activities Tracker:

Organization Name/Office Held/Leadership Status/Dates/Hours:

1. ____

____

2. ____

____

3. ____

____

4. ____

____

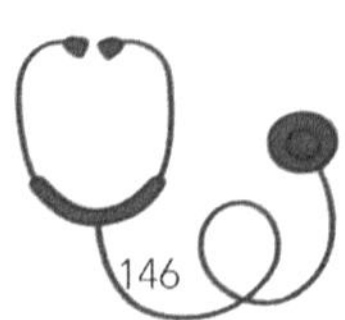

Summer Camp/Internship Tracker-Write Your Camp/Internship Details

Organization Name/Requirements/Camp Theme/Dates/Cost or Credits Received/Duties/Leadership Roles:

1. ____

____

2. ____

____

3. ____

____

Summer Camp/Internship Tracker:

Organization Name/Requirements/Camp Theme/Dates/Cost or Credits Received/ Duties/Leadership Roles:

1. ______________________________

____

2. ______________________________

____

3. ______________________________

____

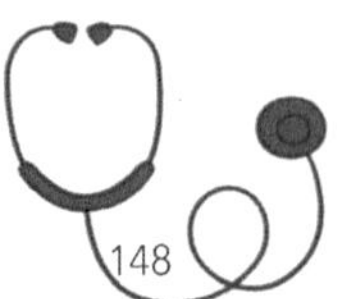

Summer Camp/Internship Tracker:

Organization Name/Requirements/Camp Theme/Dates/Cost or Credits Received/ Duties/Leadership Roles:

1. ______________________________

____

2. ______________________________

____

3. ______________________________

____

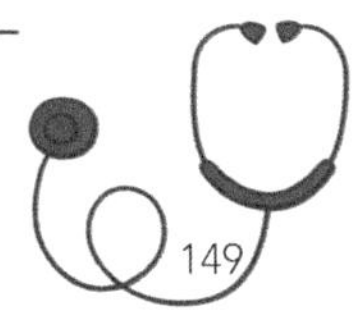

Summer Camp/Internship Tracker:

Organization Name/Requirements/Camp Theme/Dates/Cost or Credits Received/ Duties/Leadership Roles:

1. ____

____

2. ____

____

3. ____

____

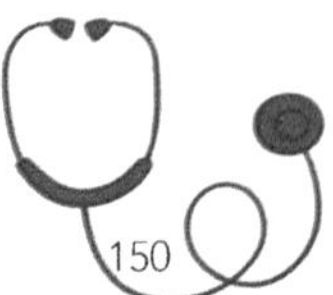

Summer Camp/Internship Tracker:

Organization Name/Requirements/Camp Theme/Dates/Cost or Credits Received/ Duties/Leadership Roles:

1. ______________________________

____

2. ______________________________

____

3. ______________________________

____

Summer Camp/Internship Tracker:

Organization Name/Requirements/Camp Theme/Dates/Cost or Credits Received/ Duties/Leadership Roles:

1. ______________________________

____

2. ______________________________

____

3. ______________________________

____

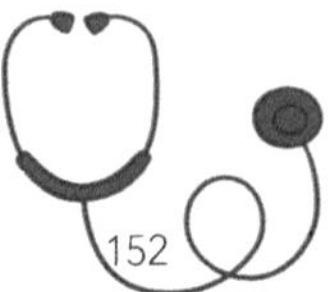

Summer Camp/Internship Tracker:

Organization Name/Requirements/Camp Theme/Dates/Cost or Credits Received/ Duties/Leadership Roles:

1. ______________________________

____

2. ______________________________

____

3. ______________________________

____

Summer Camp/Internship Tracker:

Organization Name/Requirements/Camp Theme/Dates/Cost or Credits Received/ Duties/Leadership Roles:

1. ____

____

2. ____

____

3. ____

____

Summer Camp/Internship Tracker:

Organization Name/Requirements/Camp Theme/Dates/Cost or Credits Received/ Duties/Leadership Roles:

1. ______________________________

____

2. ______________________________

____

3. ______________________________

____

"Apply, ap-
ply, apply for
scholarships!"

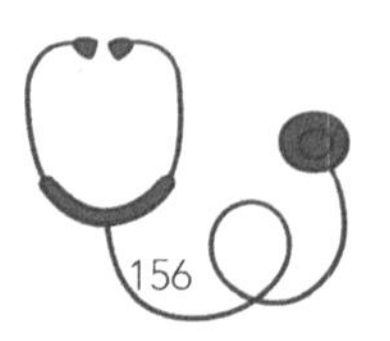

- Scholarship Doctor

Chapter Eight: **Rhea's Resources**

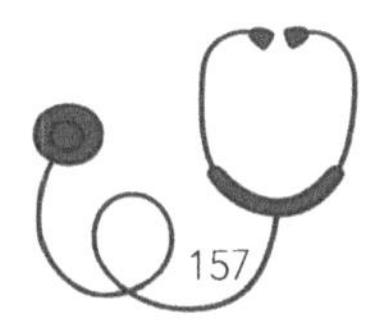

My First Scholarships

Here you will find scholarships and other resources to help you get started on your scholarship pathway.

Local Funding

Local funders are more accessible than national ones! Check the local chapters of national civic organizations. Consider student organizations; also, check with sororities and fraternities, etc. There are lots of scholarships associated with military experience, companies, unions, and/or local religious institutions. These monies are applicable for direct decedents, i.e., via parents and grandparents. Apply for the big ones, but spend your real time on the local ones!

<u>Twins & Triplets Scholarships/Discounts</u>

Carl Albert State College in Oklahoma

(Paula Nieto Twins Scholarship)

George Washington University in Washington, DC

(50% Discount for Siblings)

Lake Erie College in Painesville, OH

(Twins Alternate Scholarship Years)

Northeastern Oklahoma A&M College

(Twins/Triplets Room Fee Waiver)

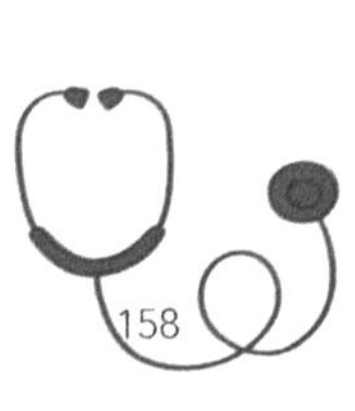

Sterling College in Kansas

(50% Discount for Each Twin)

West Chester University of Pennsylvania

(Bonnie Evans Feinberg Scholarship)

Tuition-Free Colleges

Berea College, Berea, KY: Students do not pay tuition at this Christian college but must participate in the Student Labor Program.

College of the Ozarks, Point Lookout, MO: A work college, this school foots the bill for students' tuition in exchange for 15 hours of on-campus work per week, plus two 40-hour work weeks each year during semester breaks.

Military Service Academies: $300,000.00 Scholarship

529 Savings Plan and Prepaid Tuition

You can enroll in $529 plans for as low as $15.00 per month. Also, about eight states have prepaid tuition plans. Check with your state treasurer to see if prepaid tuition is available where you live,

Monthly Scholarships

Scholarship Name: **Courage To Grow Scholarship**

Website: **www.couragetogrowscholarship.com**

General Information: Scholarship is open to juniors and seniors in high school and college students with a minimum GPA of 2.5. Visit the website for more details.

Scholarship Name: **Pulse of Perseverance Scholarship**

Website: **www.thepulseofp3.com**

General Information: Scholarship is open to high school and college students in the United States. Purchase their book in order to write a 250 word essay and submit a 60 second video. Visit the website for more details.

Video/Poetry Scholarships

Scholarship Name: **American Road & Transportation Builders**

Website: **www.artbatdf.org**

General Information: Contest is open to students in elementary school through graduate school. Contestant must submit a video on transportation infrastructure. Visit the website for more details.

Scholarship Name: **Wergle Flomp Humor Poetry Contest**

Website: **www.winningwriters.com**

General Information: Contest is open to poets of all ages and from all nations. Contestant must submit one English poem maximum of 250 lines. Visit the website for more details.

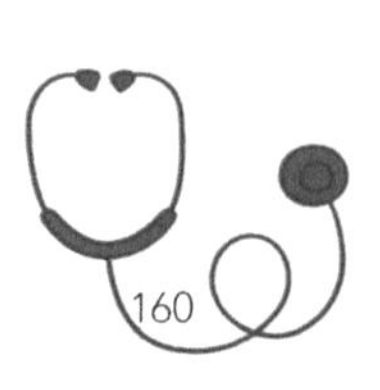

Special Circumstances Scholarships

Scholarship Name: **CBC Spouses Education Scholarship**

Website: **www.cbcfinc.org**

General Information: Applicants must be U.S. citizens or permanent residents, have a minimum 2.5 GPA, be enrolled full-time in an accredited academic institution, and reside in a district represented by a member of the Congressional Black Caucus. Visit the website for more details.

Scholarship Name: **Stephen J. Brady Stop Hunger Scholarship**

Website: **www.us.stop-hunger.org**

General Information: Scholarship is open to students in kindergarten through graduate school (ages 5-25) who have demonstrated commitment to their community by performing unpaid volunteer services impacting hunger in the United States within the last 12 months. Visit the website for more details.

General Scholarships

Scholarship Name: **ABPA Harrington-Arthur Memorial Scholarship**

Website: **www.abpa.site-ym.com/page/Scholarship**

General Information: Scholarship is open to anyone ages 13-19. Applicant must submit an essay. Visit the website for more details.

Scholarship Name: **Ben Carson Scholarship**

Website: **www.carsonscholars.org**

General Information: The Carson Scholars Fund awards college scholarships to students in grades 4 through 11 who excel academically and are dedicated to serving their communities. Visit the website for more details.

Scholarship Name: **Debbie's Dream Scholarship**

Website: **www.debbiesdream.org**

General Information: Contest is open to high school, middle school, and elementary school students across the United States. Students are provided an essay prompt to explore how they would help make a difference for stomach cancer patients. Visit the website for more details.

Scholarship Name: **Don't Text and Drive Scholarship**

Website: **www.digitalresponsibility.org**

General Information: Scholarship is open to grades 9-12 and college/graduate students. Visit the website for more details.

Scholarship Name: **Elks Scholarship**

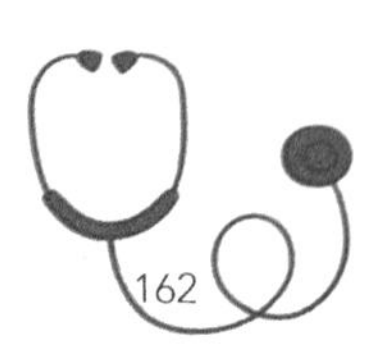

Website: **www.elks.org**

General Information: Current high school seniors, or the equivalent, who are citizens of the United States are eligible to apply. Visit the website for more details.

Scholarship Name: **Engineer Girl Essay Contest**

Website: **www.engineergirl.org**

General Information: Write about a unique topic regarding engineering. Essay should be no more than 1500 words, depending on grade level. Contest is open to individual girls and boys, ages 8 – 18, in each of three categories based on grade level. Visit
the website for more details.

Scholarship Name: **Gen and Kelly Tanabe Scholarship**

Website: **www.genkellyscholarship.com**

General Information: Scholarship is open to students in grades 9-12, college, or graduate school students who are legal U.S. residents. Applicant must submit an essay answering why they deserve the scholarship or their academic or career goals. Visit
the website for more details.

Scholarship Name: **Jack Kent Cooke Foundation Scholarship**

Website: **www.jkcf.org**

General Information: Award is open to elementary through college students. Visit the website for more details.

Scholarship Name: **Maryknoll Student Essay Contest**

Website: **www.maryknollsociety.org**

General Information: Contest is open to students enrolled in grades 6-12. Applicant must submit an essay on the topic: "Sharing Good News." Visit the website for more details.

Scholarship Name: **National Merit Scholarship**

Website: **www.nationalmerit.org**

General Information: High School students enter the National Merit Scholarship Program by taking the PSAT in their Junior year of high school. Visit the website for more details.

Scholarship Name: **SMART Scholarship**

Website: **www.smartscholarship.org/smart**

General Information: Scholarship is open to students age 18 and over who are STEM majors. Must have 1.5 years left on your degree. Visit the website for more details.

Scholarship Name: **The Prudential Spirit of Community Awards**

Website: **www.spirit.prudential.com/**

General Information: Scholarship is open to student grades 5-12. Award is based on volunteer service. Visit the website for more details.

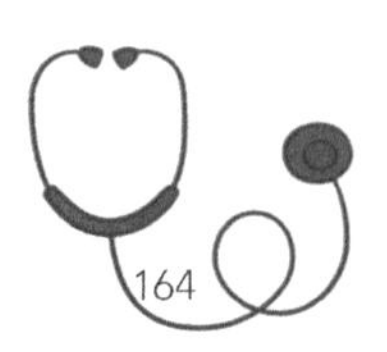

Scholarship Name: **Tylenol Undergraduate Scholarships**

Website: **www.tylenol.com/scholarship**

General Information: Annual awards for graduate students, who are interested in the healthcare field. Award is based on leadership responsibilities in community and school activities. Visit the website for more details.

Scholarship Name: **Veterans of Foreign Wars Scholarship**

Website: **www.vfw.org/Community**

General Information: The essay contest encourages young minds grades 6-8 to examine America's history, along with their own experiences in modern American society, by drafting a 300- to 400-word essay, expressing their views based on a patriotic theme chosen by the VFW Commander-in-Chief. Visit the website for more details.

Scholarship Name: **We the Future Contest**

Website: **www.constitutingamerica.org**

General Information: Contest is open to kindergarten through graduate/professional school, adults 25 years of age and older, and seniors 65 years of age and older. Visit the website for more details.

Freshman Dictionary

Listed you will find words and definitions that may be helpful for college students. This is a working document and information should be added to the dictionary.

Academic Year: It begins in August (the fall semester) and continues through the spring semester ending in May. Summer is not considered part of the academic year.

Add/drop: This is the period when changes to an original schedule can be made by either dropping a course for which you are registered and/or adding a new one.

Adjunct Professor: A broad – concept type of professor and faculty (academic staff) in higher education, at an academic rank below the highest level of professorship.

Advisor: An individual available to assist with all academic and programming concerns.

Associates Degree: **See Degrees**

Assistant Professor: A broad – concept type of professor and faculty (academic staff) in higher education, at an academic rank below the highest level of professorship.

Audit: An independent review or examination of an individual or organization for any subject matter (i.e. financial, operations, education).

Bachelors Degree: See Degrees

Bursar/Cashier: The office where students can pay bills, receive final program schedules, request refunds, and obtain book vouchers.

Career Center: A location dedicated to helping individuals find employment and learn basic skills such as interviewing, resume writing and job search.

Chair: A professor responsible for the administrative operations of an academic department.

Classification: A student's status in school (e.g., Freshman, Sophomore, etc.)

Commencement: Commencement is a public celebration recognizing either a graduation or entrance into a college/university.

Concentration: This is not a minor. A concentration is designed to permit the development of a secondary area of study, which will complement a student's major. For example, a student who is an education major may concentrate in English to prepare him/her to be an English teacher.

Core Curriculum: Specific courses which must be taken to complete a degree regardless of major.

Course Catalog: A detailed listing of courses available to students enrolled at institution of education.

Credit: A unit assigned to a course. Courses are worth anywhere from one to six credits per class.

Cumulative: Overall, to build upon, average out, or add to (e.g., a cumulative exam).

Cumulative GPA: The numerical average of all grades received from a college/university.

Curriculum Vitae: A document that showcases and highlights an individual's academic profile (courses, degrees, majors, programs).

Dean: An administrative officer responsible for a college, faculty, or division in a university.

Dean's Office: Location of the Dean, Associate/Assistant Deans in each college of a university.

Dean's List: A list of students who achieve a preset GPA at the end of an academic year.

Deferred Payment/Deferment: This is a tuition/loan re/payment plan.

Degrees:

Arts - A non-scientific branch of learning.

Science - Subjects which use observation, identification, description, of experimental investigation and theoretical explanation of a phenomena.

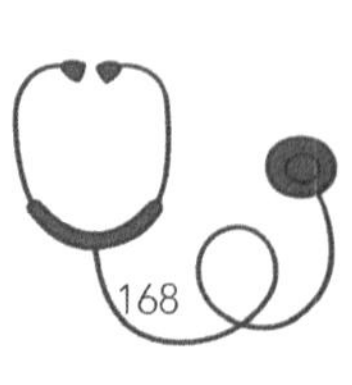

A.A/A.S - Associate of Arts or Sciences. This is a two year degree.

B.A/B.S - Bachelor of Arts or Sciences. This is a four-year degree

M.A/M.S - Master of Arts or Sciences. On average this is a two-year degree.

Doctorate - The highest academic degree awarded by a college or university in a specified discipline.

Ed.D. - Doctorate in Education Administration

J.D. - Jurist Doctorate (a law degree)

M.D - Medical Doctor

PhD - Doctorate of Philosophy (in various fields)

PsyD - Doctor of Psychology Degree

PharmD - Doctorate of Pharmacy

Distance Education: Course work that is completed outside of a formal class setting. This could be done through the internet.

Dorm: A residential building established to house students on a college or university campus.

Elective: A course a student chooses to take in addition to completing his/her major requirements.

FAFSA: Free Application for Federal Student Aid. This form determines eligibility for institutional aid and federal aid, (to include but not limited to) student loans, work study, and grants. **For more information contact your Financial Aid Office.**

Faculty: The teachers and instructors within a division; comprehensive branches of learning at a college.

Financial Aid: See FAFSA

Financial Aid Office: A unit of the college's financial services department that specializes in processing financial aid benefits for qualifying students.

Financial Aid Officer: A staff member of the financial services financial aid unit specializing in administering and processing financial aid benefits for qualifying students.

Fraternity: A male based Greek social and community based organization.

Freshman 15: A term used to describe the amount of physical weight each student gains during their freshman year due to schedule and eating habit changes.

Freshman Orientation: A required class or course for freshman students providing academic and social guidance, policy and procedure review and expectations established by the institution.

Graduate School: This is usually part of a university/college where stu dents can pursue a degree above a Bachelor's degree (e.g. a Master's degree).

Graduate Entrance Exams:

DAT - Dental Aptitude Test - Dental School

GMAT - Graduate Management Admissions Test - Masters in Business

GRE - General Records Examination - Masters in Liberal Arts including Psychology

MCAT - Medical College Admissions Test - Medical School

LSAT - Law School Admissions Test - Law School

Grade Point Average: The cumulative grade received for a semester and/or academic year(s). This is calculated by the sum of quality points for each course, divided by the amount of courses taken.

Grant: Money obtained for specific purposes (education, research, projects) that may or may not require repayment. Funding can be renewal if criteria is met and funding is available.

Honors College: A division of a college or university that offers advanced honors level courses for high achieving students.

Honor Society: An organization to which students are admitted in recognition of their academic achievement and/or their school involvement.

Incomplete: A grade given for coursework that has not met the established criteria for a pass or fail grade. Coursework or requirements has not been completed on time.

Independent Research/Study: A learning experience available if a student wishes to extend their education beyond the standard course structure of classroom activity. There is no classroom in this type of course, however a student is required to have contact with an advisor and/or participate in research in order to receive course credit.

Internship: Sometimes part of a degree requirement. This is practical experience gained through firms or organizations outside of a university.

Intramurals: Activities existing or carried on between students for healthy competition and fun (e.g., intramural athletics.)

ISBN: Textbook identification number.

IT Department: Department dedicated to the management and monitoring of computer hardware, software and programing issues.

Loans: Borrowed money that must be repaid with interest.

Subsidized: With this loan a student does not accumulate interest until repayment or during authorized periods of deferment.

Unsubsidized: With this loan, interest is charged before a student begins repayment.

Lowerclassmen: Students who are either Freshman or Sophomores

Major: An area of study or concentration selected by college or university students.

Major Requirements: Courses needed in order to satisfy graduation requirements.

Masters Degree: See Degrees

Matriculated: A matriculated student is one who has applied for and been accepted as a candidate for a degree in a specific curriculum. You must be a matriculated student to receive financial aid. **See Non-Matriculated**

Minor: A student who completes a certain number of credits (usually 18 credits) in a specified area can declare it as a minor.

Non-Degree Seeking Student: A student taking individual courses at a college or university that will not result in a degree offered by the institution. Off Campus Housing: Housing which is located near to the University. Additional information can be found through Campus Life.

Office Hours: Time set aside by a professor to meet students in his/her office. Full-time professors schedule office hours. Adjunct professors may not have office hours.

Parent Loan: Known as PLUS loans, offer additional financial funding for educational purposes to parents of students attending undergraduate or graduate schools.

Pledge: A process that students partake in order to become members of an organization (e.g. a fraternity or sorority).

Pre-Requisite: A course that must be completed before another course can be taken. **See Co-Requisite**

Pre-Registration: This is the order in which students register for classes. The earliest registration dates are reserved for currently enrolled students according to their classification.

Probation: A period of time (i.e. semester or school year) where a student is under observation and barred from specific activities due to poor academic performance and/or social behavior. Period of time can also be used to determine if student fits criteria established to join or be accepted into an academic or social organization, position (i.e. student departments, programs, fraternities, sororities)

Registrar: Office where students can request internal transfers, withdraw from classes and order transcripts.

Registration: The process by which classes are chosen and tuition is paid (or specific payment arrangements have been made). One can only register if previous balances have been settled.

Remedial Classes: Courses that are required before a student can begin their core program/degree based classes.

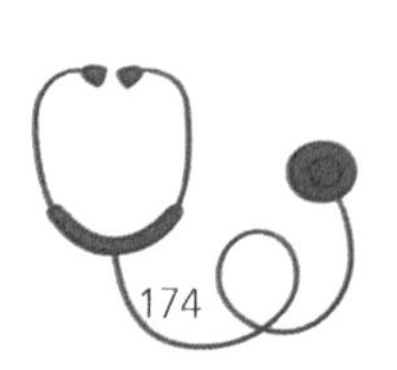

Resume: A document that highlights your educational, academic and community service/skills.

Rush Week: A week were prospective students attend informal meetings to learn about various fraternities and sororities on their college or university campuses.

Scholarship: Funding provided to students for educational purposes. Funding can be renewable if criteria is met and funding is available. Obtained through application and qualification reviews.

Semester: Represents a period of time on an academic calendar which outlines the activities and the length of courses offered during that time period. Each academic calendar has a fall, spring, summer (optional) semester.

Service-Learning: A new jazzy term for community service. Some courses may require that you participate in a specific in community service in order to complete the requirements for the class.

Sorority: A female social organization.

Student Handbook: A document issued by the college or university each school year to guide the students throughout their academic career. Handbook includes course information, requirements and outline of academic completion and graduation. Often referred to as the "Academic Bible".

Student Help Desk: An area designated on campus where students and visitors can go to get assistance (i.e. directions, operation hours, contact information).

Student ID: Normally, a photo ID issued by the college/university that allows entrance into the dorm of cafeteria or free or discounted entrance into campus events or activities. It may also be used to earn free or discounted movie tickets, airline or other travel, and meals at online and office campus business.

Student Support Services: Services offered to students to assist in their academic success (i.e. tutoring, mentorship, or counseling)

Study Abroad: The opportunity to go to school in a different country. You may live with a "host" family or in the on campus housing provided by the school of your choice.

Subsidized Student Loan: A financial loan for educational use where the government pays the interest of the loan amount while the student remains enrolled in a qualified college or university. Loans have to be repaid once the student is not enrolled in a college or university.

Syllabus: Distributed by professors at the beginning of a semester. It details what the course requires.

TA: See Teacher's Assistant

Teacher's Assistant: A graduate student who is hired to teach labs, help students with homework, proctor exams.

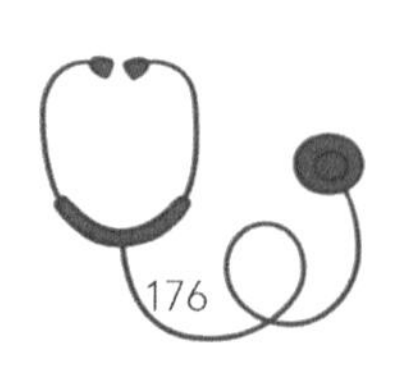

TRIO: Federal outreach and student services programs designed to identify and provide services for individuals from diverse/disadvantaged backgrounds.

Undergraduate School: Colleges or universities that offer bachelors level degrees.

Unsubsidized Student Loan: A financial loan for educational purposes which requires the student to pay accumulating interest on the loan during all periods.

Upperclassman: Students who are either Juniors or Seniors.

Transcript: An official record of the courses taken and the grades received.

Tenure: The status of holding one's position on a permanent basis without periodic contract renewals.

Work Study: Opportunities for students to work on campus (i.e. library, resource center, book store, cafeteria) while taking courses to help pay for their education (books, tuition).

Writing Center: A place where tutors assist students with papers by helping them identify common writing errors. The writing center is located in . Call for to set-up an appointment

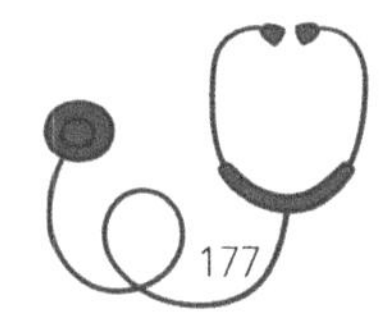

"The Scholarship Doctor is **helpful**, supportive, and informative."

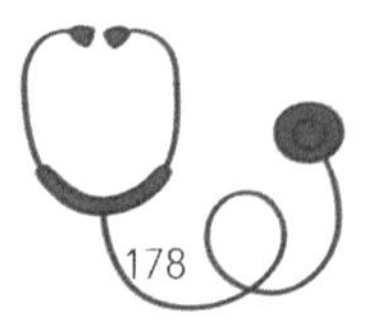

- A Driven Scholar

"I have a **FREE** degree because of Rhee!"

- It's Possible Scholar

Thank You

There are so many who I would like to acknowledge for helping me to accomplish the goal of putting my heart and passion in book form. First, I thank God, my Lord and Savior Jesus Christ, and Holy Spirit for allowing me the opportunity to do what I enjoy, every day. Secondly, thank you to my family for their support and encouragement and for keeping me grounded to do the work.

My Parents Ed and Cynthia and Grandparents Earl and Edna sowed seeds of excellence, tenacity, grit, and kindness. These seeds have grown into me being a community leader and compassionate educator. Thank you for your love, support, ingenuity, discipline, and faith. I am who I am because of you.

My beautiful sister Racquel "Kell" Watson Boumah. Kell you are so dedicated to the cause of ensuring students are successful in their quest to attend college debt free.You are also my sounding board, leaning post, and my best friend. I love and appreciate you to infinity and beyond. Friends Forever! Nothing will ever stop us!

Thank you to my super supportive and supreme marketer Brother-in-Love Joseph Boumah - your belief in me and the mission of Scholarship Solutions is immeasurable. Master Justyn Dominique Boumah, my most amazing and intelligent nephew, you are God's gift to me, our family, and the world. Joe and Just - I love you.

To my cousins Cherri, Nette, and Theressa, you all have been my prayer warriors and cheerleaders. To my brothers, friends, and protectors Darius and Godwin. To Kimberly and Angela my forever sister friends, Mama Jeanne Marsh Stahl, Uncle JJ and TT Marjorie, Mr. and Mrs. Chisolm, Ma Martha, Mrs. Brenda and Ms. Bernice, my precious Grandmother, Uncles, Aunties, and Cousins, Godmama/daddy, Godbrother/sisters, Godnieces/nephews and special friends who are family, I thank and love you all from the bottom of my heart. You have always been there and continually showed me God's love. You are so appreciated.

Mr. and Mrs. Washington and Mr. Hawkins you allowed people to learn about Scholarship Solutions, me the Scholarship Doctor, and the prescription for debt freedom. Your support has pulled 1000s of students from the demise of student loan debt. Thank you for your generous gift.

Pastors David and Vicki, Pastor Andy and Caitlin, my amazing WLCC Ministers and my entire Word of Life Family, present and past, you are the best and have helped to catapult Scholarship Solutions and me, the Scholarship Doctor, to the next level. I love and appreciate you all so much.

Certainly, it goes without saying; I thank every parent and every student who has entrusted me to help them accomplish the next level in their academic, scholarship, and college lives. If you are a purchaser or borrower, recipient of or provider of this book, thank you. If you are a member of the Scholarship Solutions Membership or a VIP Client, thank you. If you have hired me for or attended a seminar, presentation, camp, or masterclass, I appreciate you. If you have listened to me on the radio or a podcast, followed me on social media, subscribed to my newsletter, visited my website or saw me on TV, in a magazine, a billboard, or in Times Square, I am thankful for your support. Everyone - You are loved and appreciated greatly.

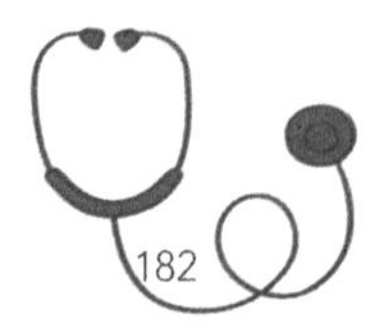

ABOUT THE AUTHOR

Rhea M. Watson, The Scholarship Doctor is Founder/CEO of Scholarship Solutions. She is a lifetime learner and educator. As a freshman entering college she was awarded one of the largest financial packages EVER offered and by the time she was a graduating senior she was actually paid $1000 per month to attend college. Additionally, during her doctoral program she was paid $1500 a month. Amazingly, her scholarship earnings have well surpassed the $300,000 mark. Rhea is an international speaker. She has presented to audiences in Egypt, England, France, Germany, Gabon, India, Jamaica, Japan, Libya, Mexico, Nigeria, Portugal, South Africa, Spain, and all across the United States of America. She has received numerous honors including, Citizen of the Year, Mentor of the Year, and Community Partnership Awards. Rhea has been featured on the TODAY show and in Forbes and Black Enterprise Magazines and is a #1 best selling author! Although her accolades are many, her greatest successes and highest honors are reflected through the students with whom she has worked.

She has been blessed to assist 100s of students enter the college of their dreams and to earn more than $200 Million dollars in scholarships. She is humbly committed to helping, “100,000 students earn a free degree, because of Rhee”.

Scholarship Solutions

10161 Park Run #150

Las Vegas, NV 89145

o:702-623-9500

w: www.myscholarshipsolutions.com

e: rhea@myscholarshipsolutions.com

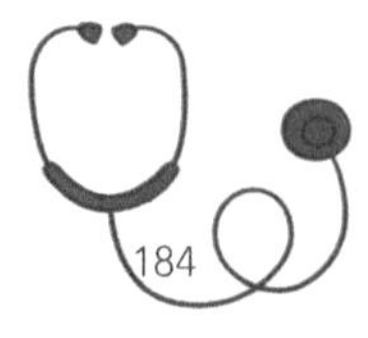

Made in the USA
Columbia, SC
14 May 2022